TOXIC

A BOOK FOR MEN

WRITTEN BY

JON PARKER

TOXIC
A Book for Men

By Jon Parker

Print version ISBN: 9781082073281

Imprint: Independently published

Written and edited by Jon Parker

Cover design by Jon Parker

Acknowledgements

There are many who made this book possible, even if by encouragement alone. You know who you are. Thanks, ya bloody savages.

CONTENTS

Introduction
READ THIS

Welcome, men. I wrote this book because men are being called toxic. Those who have no understanding of men or masculinity conflate the terrible actions of some with an entire gender, and to me that seems insane. I wrote this book because men need to know that they aren't alone. That they aren't toxic just because they are men

Before you dive in I'd like to tell you a little about this book. Firstly, it's ordered a bit differently than other books. I wanted it that way.

You'll find that every chapter designated with a whole number (1, 2, 3, etc) contains exposition about modern man, his plight and what to do about it, to include a short section at the end of each, titled *The Work.*

The Work is not intended to be a cure all, but simply the first steps that any man who needs a change, who needs to trend toward authentic masculinity, can take to begin that journey. That's really what this whole book is about.

Every other chapter, designated with a .5 (1.5, 2.5; 3.5, etc) is a short scene taken from the life of a boy who found it difficult to become a man with no true masculine influence to guide him. Maybe you'll find value in them as I do. At the very least you will see that you can come from nothing and still take control of your life.

As far as *The Work* goes, you know if you are one of the men that need it. If you are already on your journey, and you know you don't need these particular steps, read them anyway and do an audit of your life. If you're squared away there then move on and enjoy the rest of the book.

Read on!

PS: Keep reading to the end to find a sneak peek at my debut novel *Mouth Breather: Death Requires Strength*

CHAPTER 1

"Civilization comes at a cost of manliness. It comes at a cost of wildness, of risk, of strife. It comes at a cost of strength, of courage, of mastery. It comes at a cost of honor. Increased civilization exacts a toll of virility, forcing manliness into further redoubts of vicariousness and abstraction." -Jack Donovan, The Way of Men

I 've got a story I want to tell you. It's about a young man by the name of Dave. Dave was a likable enough guy - until he got on your nerves. He made friends easily, had a good sense of humor and a pretty calm demeanor. Dave smoked a lot of weed and drank a lot of booze. When he couldn't afford these things for himself, he'd beg and borrow from anyone, whether he knew them or not. The threat of violence was pretty much all that would hold Dave in check when he got into his withdrawal stage.

No matter how much actionable, clearly laid out advice or plans were given, Dave just didn't improve. He didn't climb out of his hole. Ropes were thrown, standards were set, but Dave, much like the archetypal High Chair Tyrant, refused to move, expecting everyone else to do everything for him as if he somehow deserved special treatment just for *being.*

Also much like the High Chair Tyrant, when confronted by the immovable, mature masculine, he shrank.

He shrank into the shadows long enough for the light to pass, then he was back to his old ways. Dave is still in his hole today, waiting for someone to climb down into it and install an elevator. I wonder about Dave sometimes. I wonder if he'll ever change, grow. He is taken care of by his wife, has several children, and doesn't take care of himself. I don't see any reason he should have any self-respect, and if he doesn't, how does he exist peacefully?

That's the question, right there. How does a man who isn't really a man exist peacefully? I had thought once to inquire about this, but his brain was so fried that he couldn't keep up with the conversation. If it doesn't involve the latest form of entertainment masturbation, he is unable to give any valuable insight. He can't even be bothered to care about his plight.

A man who isn't really a man cannot live a peaceful existence. This man-child is a slave to his cravings. He has no control over the call of drugs, alcohol, porn, or video games. Make no mistake, the above example is just one of *many.* There are as many different expressions of the immature masculine as there are immature men. Dave is one that I think we can all relate to on some level, though. After all, we men were all boys once.

Unlike Paul in the book of Corinthians, Dave, and all the others living an inevitably miserable existence in that immature masculinity, never put the ways of childhood behind them. They continue to talk, think and reason like children. They have aged, but they haven't become men. And it's sad.

When I was a child, I talked like a child,
I thought like a child, I reasoned like a child.
When I became a man, I put the ways of
childhood behind me.
1 Corinthians 13:11

These boys are slaves. Why do they watch porn? Because they have no choice. They'll tell you that they watch porn because they enjoy it. They'll go on about how it's not that bad of a thing to do. But they know, just like we all do on some level, that they have no choice in the matter. When the urge arises they sit down at the computer, boot it up, type in whatever fantasy they have in their minds and then see it played out on the screen. They don't know what real sexual intimacy is. Instead of going out into the world and discovering it, they opt-in for the far easier route of screwing themselves. Alone.

Why do they play video games nonstop? They have no choice. Men get their fulfillment by following their desires, affecting change, fighting for what is theirs and owning the hell out of life. Those trapped in the immature masculine can't get satisfaction from those things, because they aren't doing them. They don't know how to do them. They don't know how to kick ass and take names. Maybe no one ever showed them how. That still begs the question as to why they are staying in their hole though. Many of us had no proper masculine example, yet we still grabbed the rope and climbed out.

These guys, instead of forging their own real path in life, live vicariously through the eyes of their online avatar. They can build civilizations, take on armies and be an expert in a field - in-game. I know some choose to make a living creating or playing video games, and I'm not knocking that, but I have never known or seen a mature man that needed video games to cope with life. The ones I'm talking about need it, and they need it bad. Their self-worth is tied to how well they can push buttons.

It's the same for mind-altering substances. I enjoy a beer and cigar from time to time, as do many men that I know. However, these don't just enjoy it "from time to time." They enjoy it as often as possible within the constraints of their work schedule and budget; if they work that is. They smoke, drink, inhale, mainline, and otherwise consume substances that take the pain of reality away. Sure, it takes off the edge. It makes life a little more bearable for some. But as is typical of the immature masculine, the decision to partake in these things is utterly selfish. They don't take into account how it affects others or the health consequences of their decisions. Or they do think about these things and they just simply don't care.

I'll say it again: they are slaves. They are slaves to the substance, to the entertainment, and are therefore not in control of themselves. They don't make their own decisions, the things they are a slave to make their decisions for them. They slowly fade into nothingness, never fully realizing the darkness into which they slide. They make their way into death and mask the pain with false pleasures. As long as the road to hell is paved in gold, they will keep walking.

But why? Well, I think that it's because it's far easier to walk this path than it is to face and take on the dragons. Many must be slain, and the first one is the scariest. Rather than be the hero of their own lives, they look to others around them to do it for them. When that ultimately and inevitably fails they rationalize, telling themselves it's better to live with the dragon than it is to kill it and take back their castle.

And this is the poison of toxic masculinity. The unexpressed, repressed, masculine spirit of man, held under the water by modern societal and cultural expectations, is drowning in the depths of its own misery.

I've spoken with people in my life about my thoughts on this, and they look at me like I'm stupid. I won't lie, it can be quite frustrating. It's like people just don't get it, or don't care to. But I can't *not* get it. I can't unsee the damage that has been done to men. It's disturbing.

The prevailing mindset is causing suicides, ruined lives and just scores and scores of weak men. I know that it should circle back around, and I believe that there is a resurgence in masculinity, in strength, happening now, but it doesn't make the sight any less painful.

The Work

Look the dragon in the eyes and see your reflection exactly as you are. Admit and accept who you are right now. That's the starting point. If you are unable to admit your shortcomings then you can't accept them. If you can't accept them then you can't change them.

Be completely honest with yourself about all of the little issues that have been building up inside of you. Accept that you've let the shit pile up head high and that you're the only one who can do anything about it.

You got yourself to where you are. You can keep blaming others, or your circumstances, or any number of things, but that's what losers do. Take ownership of your life and every choice that brought you to where you are right this moment, good and bad.

You're here whether you like it or not, right? So accept it and do something about it. That's the work right now. Take stock of yourself as a man. Don't lie to yourself or hide anything from yourself. I did this for years to my own detriment. Look at yourself without judgment and know that this is when things begin to change.

Make a list of those things about you that need to change, and hold nothing back.

CHAPTER 1.5

It was Christmas morning in the country. A lonely highway snaked its way through farms and woods and over rivers and hills. There was one farm, a small thing in comparison to some others, with a blue house. In the house, a young boy was sitting at the edge of his grandparents' living room. It was sparingly decorated for the holiday, though there was a tall tree, tall to the five-year-old boy at least, that was covered from tip to base in all manner of ornaments. Underneath the tree was several presents, though he wasn't sure how many as he wasn't allowed to touch them just yet.

The boy's family sat about, idly chatting over breakfast. The boy had already finished his and was impatiently waiting for time to open his presents. He knew that the adults didn't much mind making him wait, though to him this thing called patience was anathema. Even so, he waited quietly with his back against the wall, watching his family go about their business, eating their bacon and eggs.

Succulent smells wafted through the air, but the young boy's stomach was already full. Someone was in the kitchen tending to the dinner that would be set out *later that afternoon. The boy had heard the grown-ups talking about the food they'd be eating for dinner, and to him, it sounded okay. It wasn't to be his favorite food, but at least there was food to eat.*

To his five-year-old brain, most of what the grown-ups were talking about didn't make much sense. He wanted to talk to them, to pitch into the conversation and perhaps even learn something, but they were always annoyed whenever he tried to talk to them or ask questions. And boy did he have a lot of questions. After all, there was a lot to ask about.

He wondered what some things were, what some things meant and if he could go to the creek at the back of the property and play in the water by himself; he thought he was old enough to do that. He wondered if the wasp nest on the shed had been taken care of by Grandpa, and if he might be allowed to jump on the trampoline outside by himself; he was a big boy after all. He thought to ask if there were any more snakes by the peach trees that might bite him and if he could carry the shovel around on a hunting mission. He wondered why his mother and step-father had left him and his sister with their grandparents, and why they didn't come around too often anymore. He was glad that they'd come for Christmas, of course, but he didn't know why he couldn't leave with them; that made him sad. He thought he might like to go walking down the dirt road next to the farm, the one that led back to the old, rusty red bridge. He really liked that bridge.

He had a lot of questions and very few answers. He had a lot to say, he thought, but no one was interested in hearing it, especially not when the television was on. He wasn't quite sure why, but they had no problem talking to each other with the tv on, it was only when he talked that they got annoyed. He chalked it up to grown-up-ness and left it at that. Even if he asked them they wouldn't answer, he figured, so why ask at all?

So he sat, with his back against the wall. His mind wandered from place to place as he waited impatiently for when he'd finally be allowed to open his presents. He kept thinking that he'd like to talk, to join in the conversation… But all he had to say was what interested him, and no one else cared about that. At least he had himself, and his mind, he thought. Even at five years old he was already smart enough to see that his mind was where the most fun was to be had. He could imagine real adventures in his mind. Up there he could be the hero, the explorer, the kid who got to go to the creek alone.

If no one would listen, he told himself, then he would just get good at being alone. He was more fun than the grown-ups anyway…

CHAPTER 2

"No amount of being masculine makes you toxic."
-Joe Rogan

W hen you are the only man in your life that wants to raise the standard, it's like trying to slay that dragon. To be that heroic knight who takes down the beast is something that most just won't ever attain. Let's be honest, most men don't have the inner conviction or willpower necessary to effect lasting, positive change in their lives.

That is not an excuse for the men who fail to live up to the standard set by their fellow men though. We shouldn't hope for luck to give us our due. We should expect the road to be extremely difficult. Chances are you weren't born with the willpower of a god. I know I wasn't. That means that it will take determination, perseverance and the willingness to do the difficult things to cultivate that willpower. It takes consistently making the right decisions, building up the catalog of the things you've done right. The more you do it, the easier and more automatic it becomes.

But most won't even try. Or they'll try and give up after the slightest bit of counter pressure. It is sad. I think that we all know intuitively that progress only comes through pain and struggle, but far too many men just don't want to try. It's easier to eat shit food and zombie-out in front of a screen.

Of the thousand paths that fan out before each of us, the majority will choose the one with the fewest obstacles. They'll listen to the voice that coddles them rather than the voice that urges them on toward greatness, and that is the root of toxic masculinity. That is its essence. When men don't fight to make progress they bring about their own downfall.

"Every time you repress yourself, you're taking a scoop of dirt from the spiritual ground. You can only dig so many times before you've reached 6' and your grave is ready to climb into." –Hunter Drew

How many of us, instead of marching forward into the pain and glory of becoming men, repress our impulses and desires in the name of "equality." It drives me crazy when I see this because, in the name of this ill-defined, frequently misappropriated term men are killing themselves. If not by suicide, which happens often enough as a result of repressed masculinity, then by the long, slow march into death after an unfulfilled life. They are killing their spirit more and more every day. They don't understand why other men are vigorous and strong. They can't comprehend it. It's like the darkness being unable to comprehend the light.

And the light shines in the darkness,
and the darkness did not comprehend it.
John 1:5

It's being enraged at your ineptitude and lashing out at everyone around you in an attempt to make yourself feel better. It's blaming others instead of taking ownership of your shortcomings.

It's looking for satisfaction in digital worlds, never, ever finding it. It's doing anything to get just a few precious moments away from the abyss that threatens to swallow you whole. It's not understanding why others have it better, wishing by some stroke of luck that you'd just become that man you want to be, and hating everyone else who has what you don't have.

Its smoking and drinking and eating your problems away for a moment only to have them come roaring back to life with a vengeance once the "high" wears off. It's lying in bed with the barrel of a .380 against your temple, safety off, pressure on the trigger, a split second away from ending it all. It's the monster that most are too afraid to even look at, let alone to actually fight.

"Toxic masculinity," as it has been dubbed,

isn't what they say it is. You men don't have to feel bad about existing. You don't have to listen to the shrieking banshees that say that you are evil because you're a man, because you display traits outside of the warped box they want to put you in. You are a man who is capable of so much if only you turn off the programming and tune out the insanity. You aren't toxic. Your existence isn't toxic. The only thing that is toxic about masculinity is when it's not allowed to be cultivated and expressed.

When men don't step up and claim their place in the world they are left in the muck left by the marching of the other men. No matter how many of them offer to help you, you have to decide to help *yourself* first.

Toxic masculinity, in the only form it exists, is the direct result of men not taking on the challenge that is manhood. It's a fight, every day, and a glorious one at that. It isn't easy by any stretch of the imagination, but it is worth it. And when men don't do it then they have no self-discipline. They aren't able to control themselves. The masculine impulses to forge, fight and fuck become perverted and destructive and others get hurt because of it.

I've already said that the challenge is difficult, extremely difficult, and that difficulty begins with the first step. The decision to reclaim one's own authentically masculine nature is difficult because it means facing that dragon. It means that you have to admit to yourself that you aren't right, that how you've lived up until now has been detrimental to your health and your progress. We all know intuitively when we aren't living up to our potential, but that doesn't make it any easier to admit it. Once we admit it then it becomes real. It can no longer be hidden behind or under the pleasures of the moment.

Once you see the dragon it sees you, and it wants you dead and it won't stop until you kill it or die. Once you admit that something needs to change it becomes a fight to the death.

But that's okay. The fight is necessary; it's good. Many will tell you that it isn't worth it, that you're stupid for trying. Those people are average. I can't stand them. It takes every bit of self-control that I possess to not tear into them up one side and down the other.

Modern man has every opportunity to make himself better, stronger, more capable, but he just doesn't do it. Well, most of the time. You, reading this book, might just be the exception to that.

I hope that you are. The more masculine men there are, the more likely a true resurgence can take place. The light should burn. That's what it was made to do. It's a tragedy when a bright light is hidden, or snuffed, or otherwise made not to shine.

The prevailing mindset is that, as I'll talk about more than once in this book, the natural light need not shine when the artificial light is so bright. The problem is that it's not reliable. The sun is reliable.

In the same way that the sun was created to

shine, so too was the masculine spirit. It is power-ful. It is strong. It is *not* in and of itself "toxic." It becomes toxic when it is boxed up and stored in the closet, made to fester in the dark.

The Work

Consider how many times in recent history you've been a good boy. How many times were you offered confrontation and you sat down instead of facing it like a man?

Do you more often hold your tongue or speak your mind? There is a time and a place for both, certainly, but our docility as men has become such, in large part, that we don't speak up anymore. We're afraid that we'll be browbeaten by those ever more tolerant than us.

The self-proclaimed *new nobility* casts judgment more viciously than many want to admit, or face, and so they remain quiet.

The first step for you, Man, on this journey, is that you must ask yourself how much you are prepared to lose to revive the masculine spirit within you. You'll lose friends, for sure. You might lose your job. I've known men who've lost their marriages in pursuit of authentic masculinity.

Are you prepared to lose it all to regain that heretofore elusive thing called *masculinity?*

You may lose nothing. You may lose it all. At the very least expect people in your life to begin falling away, and expect your inner world to change drastically.

Now, the work. **The next time you feel like**

something isn't sitting right with you, speak up. If someone is challenging you, stand your ground.

When I was in the police academy I earned several nicknames. Mack truck, juggernaut, and gorilla are the three that I remember. I always thought this was very telling because more than anything these nicknames represent who I am on the inside. I'm of a decent size in body, but I'm not huge by any means.

These nicknames were earned because no matter who it was in my class that had a problem, I didn't back down from them. My class was full of some cocky bastards, too. I think a certain level of arrogance is necessary for any potential candidates for police departments.

Anyway, you've got to be that Mack truck, the juggernaut or the gorilla. You must be the immovable object that others break upon.

Don't worry about being all that *yet*, just take this thing one step at a time. You can go ahead and keep reading, but remember that this step *cannot* be skipped. No matter where you are in the book or your daily life, *do not* skip this step.

CHAPTER 2.5

"I told you I just went to go get some fucking weed!" her husband yelled at her.

"Bullshit, you son of a bitch! I know you're fucking around on me!" her rage was palpable, permeating the atmosphere, penetrating the doorway into the boy's room.

He tried to block out the noise by covering his head with his pillow, but he could still hear them fighting. He knew it would go on for hours, into the morning even, just like it always did. He hated it. He hated them, sometimes, too. They couldn't stop drinking and snorting and smoking long enough to see the effect they were having on the boy.

He wondered if he'd be better off if he'd stayed living with his grandparents. They always treated his sister better than they treated him, but at least they weren't violent and angry all the time. Sure, Grandpa used to make him get a switch off the peach tree when he was in really deep trouble, and he'd take as long as he could in doing so. He'd trudge back into the house with it, heart beating wildly in fear at the upcoming pain.

He hated the man in those days. After all, who

switches a six-year-old? But that was when Grandpa drank a lot. He'd load the boy and his sister up and drive over to the nearest town where he'd pull through the drive-through and order the same thing every time, a pint of black velvet, all for himself. He'd get drunk before Grandma got home from work and any misstep brought pain, and lots of it.

Thankfully he'd found Jesus and quit drinking cold turkey. He became a different man after that. Still a worker, still grouchy a lot, but more pleasant to be around. He started taking the boy fishing, which were some of his favorite memories. Every fishing trip started before sunrise, of course, and they always made a pit stop to pick up some slim-jims before hitting the water. They'd go to lakes all over the area, pulling in whatever they could get to bite. A lot of it went back in the water, but some of it went home for dinner, and those were the best dinners. Especially since they didn't involve any of that nasty boiled okra. Fried was good, boiled was like eating slimy boogers.

The boy lay there in the dark, trying to be any-where but in his own life. He didn't think that this is how kids were supposed to live. None of the kids in school ever talked about their parents acting the way his did. But of course the boy had no friends, so why would they tell him anything at all? He was weird and quiet. He wanted friends but he couldn't get over him-self enough to try. Besides, letting people in, letting them see what his life was like outside of school, that would only scare them off. He didn't want the embarrassment of it, and neither did he want to embarrass his parents, because, despite everything, he knew that he was supposed to honor his father and mother. That's what he was taught. Even if the man wasn't his real father and his real father didn't care enough about him to be there, he was taught to do right by them.

He loved school, even though he had no friends. The food was better than at home and more consistent. He could always get a slice of pizza or a cheeseburger. He always got a mound of dill pickles, too. Those were his favorite. Lunch at school was his favorite time of day. Even though he had no friends he still relished the energy that was present in the lunchroom. He loved to listen to the other kids talk, to hear what normal life was like.

He knew that others had it worse than him, and so tried not to pity himself too much. When he was feeling particularly bad he found that the woods helped him forget his life. The quite, the solitude, the peace... They made him happy. He wanted to play video games, like the other kids, but his parents were poor, and what little money they had they spent on drugs and alcohol. Somehow, they always seemed to have enough money to have those things in near-constant supply.

He lay there, in the dark, listening to screaming and cursing and rage and violence; to smashing and hitting and breaking; alone in his room and his mind and his life, wishing he were anyone else but him.

CHAPTER 3

*"There is one rule, above all others,
for being a man. Whatever comes, face it
on your feet." -Robert Jordan*

Men have retreated. In all the ways that matter, men as a whole have retreated. Why? Because they've been made to feel bad about their masculinity by their mothers, sisters and wives, friends, co-workers... Sometimes intentionally, often enough inadvertently. This isn't the early days of man where survival depended on the savagery of men. The things required of the men of old simply aren't required of most men alive today. For the first time in human history, men don't need to be masculine to live. And men see this, we know it. We understand that what was required of our ancestors is not required of us. This, coupled with the feminist call to set aside all things that make men and women different, and with the cries of wrongs done in decades past, has served to pacify the majority of men.

Once, long ago, the dragon was on the horizon and the knight, the hero, would go out and destroy it, making the castle safe once more. Now, the only dragon that needs to be slain is within each of us. Once men would conquer the enemies outside and within themselves, often the enemy within had to be defeated to become strong enough to face the enemy at the gates. But when the only enemy most men face is within them, and the man can waste away in cheap, ignorant bliss because there are no enemies at his doorstep, then he often just sees no good reason to go through the pain of becoming a man.

And so, men have retreated. They've retreated into their "man caves" where women aren't allowed until their wife knocks on the door and demands to be allowed entry or she'll "cut them off" from the pleasures offered by her femininity. They've retreated into safe spaces and circle jerks where they rage, with each other, against the patriarchy and all things masculine.

They aren't willing to fight for what that masculinity offers. They look at masculine qualities and are disgusted. They abhor things like strength, vigor, logic, competition, and aggressiveness. And the worst thing about it is that it wasn't the men that made this decision, it was the boys that each of them used to be, that each of them still is. From an early age, boys are taught to sit down and shut up and to be good little girls. If they don't behave like all the other little girls then they are treated with contempt.

Our sons are taught that their energies

Jon Parker

are toxic, that their adventurous impulses are dangerous and that they are bad if they don't listen and go along with the status quo. Of course, when I say "our sons" I am talking collectively. My sons are not made to feel this way. Why should they be? Why would I want to teach them that their very existence is the root of all evil in this ever more feminized culture?

I wouldn't. I don't. I won't.

I won't teach them that they are anything less than the beginnings of great men. Because that is what they need to know. To make it, boys need that validation. They need to know that growing into a physically, mentally and spiritually developed man is a goal worth attaining. And they need to hear that from a physically, mentally and spiritually developed man.

It's a cycle of death perpetrated by the cult of it. The masculine spirit is being killed off in one man at a time by this extremely destructive narrative, starting when they're boys and ultimately, rapidly, culminating in the feminization of a huge swath of the generation. For boys especially, its much easier to build a new world in-game than it is to place a cornerstone in the real world. The strength and courage it takes to do the hardest thing instead of the easiest thing used to be revered and encouraged and instilled in boys, but now the easiest thing they can do is made readily available to them and accepted; even expected.

It seems that moderation is steadily becoming

a disappearing value. Why moderate when one can have it all? Why hold back when it's only my life that I'm ruining?

Those questions may sound silly, but I guarantee that people are asking them of themselves. In large part, people just don't give a damn if they are living a low-quality life overall as long as they get their little pleasures. The big picture doesn't matter; the future doesn't matter. I ask men why they don't do anything about their obesity and am told, "I like eating. If I'm going to die early then at least I'll have done it with a full belly and a smile on my face."

The problem there is they didn't earn that smile. They stuff their faces every day with the worst food you can think of in the name of their happiness. What's worse is that they know that this happiness only lasts a moment. It only lasts until the meal is gone and the tastes have disappeared. Then they feel bad about their lack of self-control and try to mask those feelings with some other substance that'll give them a dopamine rush.

The process is repeated every day. It is the literal definition of insanity. Yet it continues unabated save for the occasional foray into "healthy eating" and dropping 15 pounds only to gain it back and then some.

The way of masculinity is broken. It is hated on, lied about, misrepresented and, above all, repressed. There is a deep-rooted desire within us to push boundaries, to explore and to discover. We have to see what is over the next rise, what the ground looks like from the top of the mountain, what the water feels like. We feel pulled to leave the trail and see what else lies in the wilderness.

But for too long we've been told there is nothing left to see there, nothing worth the effort. As a result, our way is broken, we are broken, and nothing can change that but a return to cultivating the wild heart of man.

The Work

Don your armor, grab your sword and face down your enemies. Recognize them for who and what they are, and prepare to do battle.

You've listed out those qualities about yourself that you want to change. No matter what others tell you, people can and do change all the time. They may have tendencies toward certain behaviors, but they can still change. I've done it, and you will do it too if you keep reading this book and doing The Work.

You've stood up for yourself. You've experienced what it feels like to have that fire burning inside once more. You will continue to do so. You will stand your ground when others push you. You will be the strong redwood in the storm.

Now it's time to destroy your doubts. **Set aside one hour today and use it solely to work out.** Whatever form that takes for you, just do it. Run, lift, bike, hike, climb, swim, hell, walk if that's what you've got to do.

And don't take it easy, either. *Really* hit it for that hour. Push your limits. Only you know what pushing yourself feels like. We're all at different stages, after all. You are the only one who can hold yourself accountable in your heart. You'll know if you're failing yourself and you'll have to live with it.

So spend an hour today pushing yourself physically. If pushing yourself means a brisk walk, that's fine as long as you are *actually* working hard at it. It might mean that you run for the whole hour, or do calisthenics, or any number of things.

If you are reading this book because you need *The Work* then do it. No excuses.

CHAPTER 3.5

"Move bitch!" Wyatt said as he came down the bus aisle toward the back. The boy's girlfriend, cute as could be but strange nonetheless, lay across the aisle in two seats. She sat up quickly to get out of his way. The boy, however, didn't like Wyatt's tone.

"Wyatt, how about you shut your fucking mouth before I shut it for you," he said. So arrogant was the boy that he didn't turn to watch as Wyatt came back up the aisle the few steps that he'd made it to punch him in the back of the head. The boy was jaded, tired of the emotional roller coaster that was his life. He'd long ago become an asshole, especially to those who were rude to his girlfriend. After all, who would be her white knight if not for him?

The punch didn't really hurt his head, but it did hurt his ego. And it pissed him off. His head jerked forward without warning. Anger was just one of those emotions that he always seemed to feel. His fuse was short and words were cutting. This time he didn't use words, though. That split second of shock that comes after getting punched without warning wore off quickly and the boy stood up in his bus seat and faced Wyatt. They were teammates on the football team, but that didn't matter to the boy right then. He hopped over the back of his bus seat. Rage flooded through him and he jumped without thinking. He stepped and dove into Wyatt, thinking to tackle him back into his seat and beat the shit out of him.

Unfortunately for the boy, Wyatt weighed more than the boy thought and didn't move nearly as far back as the boy thought that he would. What he did do was start wailing on the boy's head, shoulders, and back. The boy hit back, striking him in his legs and sides, but he soon realized that this was a losing battle. With Wyatt's arm wrapped around his head, he had to push with all his might to get loose. He backed up a step and turned his head to see the Assistant Principal on his way down the aisle. Apparently, he'd been close enough to hear what was happening.

The boy tried to get back in his seat but the AP pointed at him and called him and Wyatt toward the front of the bus. "My office, now," he said with a stern look on his face. Emotion began to well up in the boy, his face getting hot. He'd never lost a fight before, or whatever that was. This tussle had ended with him in the losing category, taking more pain than he'd given, and now he was beginning to feel shame.

Anger was one of the emotions he dealt with daily, and it got him into fights more often than most, but it wasn't the only feeling that seemed to be nearly ever-present in his life. Just as fast as his anger was subsiding it was being replaced by the empty feeling that he hated so much. Everything about him deflated into a depressive state.

Instantly sadness overtook him and he felt his eyes begin to burn. He hated this about himself, too. Among most of his other qualities... The only thing he liked about himself was his imagination and sense of humor. Most people didn't like either of those things of his, but he did, and that was all that mattered to him.

As he walked toward the front of the bus, followed closely by Wyatt, the boy fought back tears. He didn't know how to explain it but he'd always thought that he felt everything more fully than those around him. Just from how they acted, the looks in their eyes, how they laughed... He knew, somehow, that they weren't feeling things like he was feeling them.

It was great when he was enjoying something because he was really enjoying it. But unfortunately it also applied to negative emotions, and when they rose he could not help but want to end everything, such was the pain. He thought he was weak, because of that, and that made him feel all the worse. His rage, his bravado, his sharp tongue, all very real, but they paled in comparison to the depression.

And so he wasn't able to hold back the tears indefinitely. He loathed himself for that, for his weakness, his overflowing and uncontrollable emotion, for nearly everything. He often thought of suicide. Sure it was said to be the coward's way out, but to him, sometimes being a dead coward seemed like it might be better than living in such self-hatred for the rest of his life.

CHAPTER 4

A man may conquer a million men in
battle but one who conquers himself is, indeed,
the greatest of conquerors. -Buddha

What would you do today if you didn't have yesterday as a template? I'd bet that you'd do whatever seemed interesting; go whichever way the wind blew you. You'd probably do something you've never done before. That would be strange, right? How many times have you done the same things day in and day out?

In our rush toward the finish line, it seems that we like to automate processes. Like a machine, we follow the same steps, the same plans, the same routines, every day. Maybe your day looks something like this:

1. Wake up too late

2. Quickly brush your teeth

3. Swiftly take a dump

4. Throw on whatever clothes you can find

5. Grab whatever food is easiest to eat on the way out the door

6. Get to the job

7. Stress out all day because you hate your job

8. Spend several hours doing anything other than your job

9. Go home

10. Eat whatever is easiest to make

11. Watch TV

12. Stay up too late

13. ....

I know some of you reading this right now are thinking how similar that generic list is to your actual circumstances. Maybe it's different for some of you. Maybe not. Either way now is the time that you take a hard look at your daily activities.

I'm not going to go in-depth about how to do that right here. It is pretty self-explanatory. Recount what you've done each day this week and figure out if anything was out of the norm for you. If there wasn't anything new, why not?

Some of you may be wondering why in the hell it even matters. The truth is, maybe it doesn't. After all, we already know that men need not be warriors any longer, we need not be adventurers or explorers or vigorous or powerful, not to survive in modern society at least. The vast majority of men can get by being average. The average outnumber the exceptional by so grand a margin that they are actually making headway in eliminating real men from the world.

And therein lies the problem. I see it; we all do. What's needed is for men to make an unapologetic return to masculinity. If you're reading this book then chances are you feel it in your heart, as I do. I am not ashamed to admit this, and neither should you be. Men *need* to be able to revive their masculine natures without the lies of modern society eating away at them.

There is no reason to be ashamed or to be guilty for being a man. It's easy to do what society tells you to do, but it is also detrimental to both your long term well-being as a man and the future of unapologetic masculinity itself. But we're told we should be apologetic, grovel at the feet of those who are weak. We're told that real men aren't needed anymore.

I'll say it again: you can most likely live as an average man for your entire life. But there is a subset of us men that can't fucking stand the thought of that. I, personally, abhor the idea of living an average existence. There is nothing in that kind of life for me. I'm not saying I'm the best or the smartest or the fastest or the strongest or the most capable, but I don't have to be. Great men see a goal and chase it relentlessly.

I see what I want. I know where I want to be. I see who is in first place and I will chase them off the edge of the fucking Earth.

Maybe it doesn't matter to you. If that is the case, put down the book and go on about your average life. If it does though, and I believe that to be the case for most of you, then now is the time to make the change.

I ask you again: What would you do today if you didn't have yesterday as a template?

You see, far too many men are just recycling. They recycle the same tired old things day after day, never experiencing anything new. Don't be one of those men. Don't just be another average mother fucker. Get out and make yourself better. It's your choice, every day, to keep going the same way you've been going, or to step off that beaten path and blaze a new trail.

What will you do?

The Work

Get a notebook or a whiteboard or a laptop or whatever you like to write with and go somewhere that you can think uninterrupted. Put your headphones in/on or sit quietly; whatever it takes to get into the right head-space.

Take a look at the last 30 days of your life. What has your daily life been like? How many days stand out? Can you differentiate between the last few Wednesdays, or does every day blur into the next one? Are your days the same, day in and day out?

Make a conscious effort, as soon as you are able, to do something new; something that you'll remember in a few weeks. It doesn't have to be expensive or far away from where you live. If you take the time to look I'm certain that you'll find something to do that you've never done before. Do it. No excuses. Get out of the house and do it.

Go this weekend or today. Hell, go now if you can manage it. Go see something you've never seen before, walk where you've never walked before. It's really simple, you just have to have the will power to change yourself for the better, and this is one step on that journey. Ultimately you need to make this a regular thing. Weekly, monthly, quarterly, whatever you can manage.

You and I both know that change doesn't come from doing the same thing over and over again. Re-cycling the same old shit is going to give you the same results every time. It's time for something new.

Pretend you don't have a template to go off of and start fresh. What will you do without yesterday's influence?

CHAPTER 4.5

"Dude why is my body vibrating?" the boy asked.

"Bro, I told you it wasn't fake! You just smoked real weed!" laughed Wes.

"Yeah I can smell it in my mouth, but...." the boy trailed off. "This feels different than before..."

"I still think it's crazy that your mom showed you how to roll a joint..." Wes said slowly. "Eh, I guess it's not that crazy..."

"Where did you get this shit?" the boy asked dazedly.

Wes choked up, laughing, "Dude you are so high!" His eyes were red and his face even more so.

"Ahhhhh... I'm hungry. Where're the snacks? And drinks? And chips?"

"Uh... kitchen."

The boy rose unsteadily to his feet and walked into the living room through the kitchen, forgetting all about his munchies. He heard someone making noise in the living room and had to check it out. As he walked through the doorway between the kitchen and living room he stopped, catching a glimpse of someone behind the catty-cornered couch. He just saw hair at first but when he fell onto the back of the couch he saw Wes's cousin. He didn't know her name, just that she was strange.

He stared at her for a moment, not quite able to make out what she was doing. She had a small red gas jug in her lap with a black spout coming out of the top of it. Her lips rested around the end of the spout, her cheeks sucked in. A few moments later she released her mouth's grip and sat back into the corner where the couch met the wall. She grinned a stupid grin.

"What are you doing?" the boy asked.

She didn't respond at first, just stared at him blankly. When she did answer it was quiet and slow, "I'm huffing gas. You want some?" The boy crinkled his nose, the smell of gasoline invading his senses.

"Nah, I'm good," he said. He felt really stoned, but the girl looked like she was on the dark side of the moon. But no, he felt like he was on the dark side of the moon... So she must be on Jupiter or something. He nodded to himself as if he'd had some divine revelation, eyes wide, mouth hanging open. He rolled off of the back of the couch, then onto the floor, and stumbled to his feet.

Just then he heard a guitar. That was what had drawn him into the living room, to begin with! He turned to see Keith sitting in front of the old, dusty fireplace, black and white electric guitar resting on his leg. He was strumming away like a professional. His skill was amazing. He didn't know Keith could play guitar! Every time he'd picked up the thing before he was absolutely terrible! To think, all this hidden talent on display before him now.

The boy smacked his lips, realizing how dry his mouth was. Ah yes! Snacks and drinks! He turned back toward the kitchen, only to end up sitting on another couch on the other side of the large living room. He wasn't sure how long he sat there, but eventually, he began feeling more...normal. The guitar playing started to sound more mediocre and he was released from its spell.

Finally, he could go get some snacks. He rose to his feet, a little more steadily than last time, and walked toward the refrigerator. Once through the door, he saw Wes still sitting at the table. He opened the fridge only to find condiments and a loaf of bread. No drinks or snacks existed therein. He was devastated. Steeling himself, he grabbed the loaf of bread and the mustard. His mouth was so dry that any consumable, liquid-like material would have to do. He took out a slice of bread, rolled it up into a ball and squirted some mustard on top before popping it in his mouth. It was better than he thought it would be.

He made it through half the loaf before grabbing a dirty cup out of the cupboard and filling it with tap water. He chugged the odd-tasting water and set the cup in the sink. Just then Wes looked over at him.

"Hey man, I'm loading a bowl... You want some?"

CHAPTER 5

A man must stand erect, not be kept erect by others. -Marcus Aurelius

Modernity wants men to constrain themselves. It wants men to take their masculine energy and put it into a nice, hideable box, and to throw away the key. Others expect us to collar ourselves for their benefit; to restrain our natural mode of being to fit within their view of how the world should be.

We know that. We know the problem. It has been made ever more evident in recent years with the rise of third-wave feminism and their not quite masculine "allies." I put that in quotations because to be allied with such a disgusting, destructive ideology as third-wave feminism is revolting. The ideology itself with its misconceived notions of what it is to be a masculine man leaves enough of a bad taste as it is. There's a special place in the dirt for men who refuse the mantle, the honor, of masculinity in favor of collaring themselves and handing the leash to their "over-ladies."

They tear down the idea of men in roles of leadership, neglecting the fact that men in roles of leadership is how we got to this point in history, living in the most egalitarian society that has ever existed, for better or worse.

Masculine virtues brought about the exploration of the world and the stars; the industrial revolution; the Enlightenment; the technological era.

Masculine virtues, masculine men, built the world into what it is and are now expected to hand over the kingdom because how we live, the things we believe in and uphold, are not compatible with the new cadre of the overly sensitized and feminized. In the Oppression Olympics, only the losers win.

As Jack Donovan, author of *A More Complete Beast*, puts it,

"In the space of a few hundred years, the noble morality of the sovereign has been exchanged for the ignoble morality of the squeaky wheel."

The people have begun to revere weakness, impotence, and hedonism. They despise strength, power, and discipline. The world has been turned on its head and that which was once held in high regard is now a blight on the history of humanity in the eyes of these, the weak, the ignoble.

Those who oppose the prevailing mindset must be destroyed in any way possible. Of course, it's not like it used to be. They don't kill the ones they hate, they just mock them into obscurity. In reality, their weapons are weak and their wills are weaker, but in the name of an ill-defined fairness men have let them take the helm.

The "problem" is that beasts don't do well with collars. The beast with a thriving spirit won't allow a collar to be placed around his neck. He won't allow another to claim mastery over him. No matter how many rise against him, no matter the strength of the weapons, he will die before he is enslaved.

This is where we are. A movement of men refusing to back down is rising, men who refuse the collar - who refuse to bow. They've seen the darkness brought on by voluntary enslavement and they've realized that it was indeed voluntary. They have begun to see that the masculine power within is not a detriment to modernity, but rather the creator of it. The masculine spirit is not something to be hated or fearful of. It should be embraced, cultivated, and expressed with confidence, especially now in the face of such a hateful enemy.

It was the willful stepping down of men that got us to where we are and I believe it will take the willful return of men to affect things positively.

No amount of self-loathing for past wrongs is going to fix anything, so clapping that collar around your neck is not good in any way. It's cowardly and detrimental to *everything.*

All that has been built cannot be maintained by willingly imprisoning ourselves. Sometimes it isn't the outside enemy, but the man himself, that creates his own prison. The cycle, likely begun by someone with power over us, is inevitably perpetuated by us when we don't begin to make good decisions. When we allow others' negative influence to have such an effect on our lives that we hide away in our cells like good little emasculated prisoners.

This has to stop. Men must grasp the reality that walling off the beast helps absolutely no one in the long run. Only by being true to who we are as men can we hope to shift the tide back in our favor. Compromise is necessary sometimes, but men have begun to compromise on the very nature of their souls. This path can only ever lead to ruin.

Of course, ruin is exactly where *they* want masculine men to end up. They want to ruin men, tame men, break men's spirits, and collar men. Collared like a dog, ready to be shocked at a moment's notice for barking too loudly, and put down for a bite. But some few men figure it out. They realize what's been taken from them. They see the way things were and feel like the rug has been pulled out from under them. The nobility of the beasts of the wild, who's nobility comes from its own nature and living according to it.

"You realize, not intellectually, but viscerally, metaphorically - and thus Truthfully - with those enteric gut-brain neurons, with your own heart and your own balls, that [the] beast's nobility lies in its violence and power and murderous malice, that its regal virtue is its unthinking allegiance to its own will and dominance and that it wears its crown with taut but unstrained neck muscles, that it holds its scepter without ambivalence, that it takes Rome as an osprey takes a fish, by sovereignty of nature..."-From Sanction I, by Roman McClay

We haven't been living according to our natures, and it is killing us. You can't long toy with the foundation of your being without utterly destroying yourself.

Like a house of cards, you fall to nothingness with the slightest breeze. Nothing sturdy can be built on shaky ground, for solid materials, strong materials, carry a weight that will bear down mightily on a foundation that isn't strong enough to hold it. Meaning, a man who hasn't built his house upon the solid foundation of his masculine nature will surely be unable to shoulder the burdens of manhood. He must take off the collar about his neck, or never allow it there, to begin with. The beast's nobility doesn't allow for a collar.

The Work

Take off the collar and throw it away. Now is when you stop accepting what others tell you, simply for the sake of getting by.

Stop listening to the voices of others and turn inward. What is your heart saying; what is God saying? This quote is elsewhere in this book, but it bears sharing here as well:

"None of us will ever accomplish anything excellent or commanding except when he listens to this whisper which is heard by him alone."
—*Ralph Waldo Emerson*

You alone know the calling in your heart. Refuse to be collared, controlled, by what others do and say. It's difficult to stand on your own when you're used to being held erect by others, but you must. Listen to the voice inside, really listen, today.

Take one hour today to be silent and listen. No phone, no books, no radio, no internet. Just you.

You aren't focusing on exercising, or making a list, or any destination in particular. Just get somewhere alone.

Personally, I love going into the woods near the lake north of town. There is a long wooden bridge that goes over several creeks that run into the lake. It's mostly used for biking the trails out there, but I just love the peace and solitude that I find there. I can really listen to what's happening inside and make appropriate course corrections if needed.

You might not have a favorite place like that, but that's okay. If you do have one, go there. If you don't then just drive, radio off, windows down if you enjoy that kind of thing. Even better, if you've got a motorcycle go ride that. There's nothing quite like getting out of city limits on a bike, just you and the road and the wind.

You'll notice that I'm not trying to box you in with any of this work. I'm a huge proponent of individuality and doing what works for you. So do what works for you! Go somewhere quiet and peaceful and *hear* what is going on inside of your heart and soul.

Don't skip this step. I know it may be hard to do, but you must. Most people can't go an hour without checking their phones, let alone without any distractions at all.

Don't be like those people. Do the work.

CHAPTER 5.5

He strode the lonely streets alone. The boy... that's what his mother had always called him. It's how he had thought of himself for so long; just a boy. But now he was alone. Now he had to survive on his own. He had to figure out how to be a man. He had no idea what it meant, not really, but he did know that he was hungry, and he had to eat.

His scrawny frame did nothing to intimidate others, but it did make him...invisible. He found that he was quite adept at getting into stores and getting back out of stores without being bothered by anyone. They never noticed when his pants and his pockets were full of their merchandise, either. He didn't feel good about stealing, but he had no other way to eat.

Fifteen was awfully young to have left home, but he'd done it. He wasn't thriving, but he was surviving. He was having fun, too. In spite of the difficulties and the worry and the doubt, he was doing okay. He'd even found a girlfriend, for a moment. It had quickly turned to shit. He thought he'd fallen in love, but realized soon enough that it had been little more than lust. They'd had a lot of fun and a lot of sex. They'd said the words to each other, and he thought he'd meant them. Trouble was, she had meant them.

When he told her the truth she had threatened suicide. It broke his heart but he couldn't lie about it, it wasn't in his nature. She didn't do it. She didn't kill herself, which he was extremely thankful for. He didn't know what he'd do if he was the cause of this beautiful girl's death. He saw the long term and knew she had the potential to become something, someday. His shoes scuffed the pavement, creating a sound that was comforting to him. Leaves littered the ground, strewn about by uncaring winds. Autumn.

He continued walking, up the long hill to the grocery store at the top. Hopefully, he'd be able to get in and out again, without being noticed. He didn't take too much from the grocery store, not wanting his activities to be evident. When he got to the parking lot he noticed that there were only a couple of cars there. He'd have to be extra careful. Fewer cars meant fewer people to distract employees. He strode confidently through the automatic double doors, black hood over his shoulder-length, auburn hair, hands in his hoodie pockets.

There was nothing for it but to be done as quickly as he could. He did his best to not look suspicious, but the cashier watched him closely nonetheless. He walked to the back of the store, where the refrigerated foods were, and grabbed his favorites. A bottle of sweet tea and a package of pepperonis. He could easily conceal these things and knew that no cameras were watching him. He shoved the tea bottle in his waistband and the pepperoni package in his cargo pocket. He wandered around the aisles for a bit, trying to pretend that he was looking for something. In one of the aisles, he came across another of his favorites, a chocolate pudding pie. He snagged one of those and put it in his other pocket.

The cashier appeared, then, and said, "Can I help you find something?" Her eyes were narrowed and he knew the jig was up.

"No, I was just looking for something..." he replied, hands once again in hoodie pockets. "Looks like you don't have it." He took his cue to leave, hoping she hadn't called the cops.

Back at the front of the store, the double doors opened for him once more. This time the parking lot was different though. A black and white police cruiser sat, still running, right out front. The officer was just getting out when the boy exited the store. Just as he was rounding the front of his car the boy bolted.

"THAT'S HIM!" came a scream from behind him, undoubtedly the voice of the cashier.

He didn't stop to see for sure, just ran. He was sure that he knew these streets well enough to stay hidden. There were plenty of places to hide that these small-town cops wouldn't, or couldn't, search. He ran down the hill, between two large, old brick buildings, into a dark alley. He could stay here for a while.

He opened the chocolate pudding pie and bit into it. The glazed exterior with the chocolate interior almost made him smile. It tasted so good. He dropped the package on the ground and opened up the tea, guzzling it down quickly. He threw the bottle to the other side of the alley and pulled out a recently stolen pack of smokes *as the bottle bounced around on the pavement. He looked back between the two buildings he'd run through, and up and down the alley, and saw no one.*

He pulled out his lighter, also lifted, and lit a cigarette, taking a long drag, holding it in for a few seconds before exhaling. The nicotine flooded his body, lessening the tension on his frayed nerves. He leaned back, pressing his back up against the wall, and looked up at the night sky. He wondered where he'd sleep tonight.

CHAPTER 6

*The superior man is he who develops, in harmonious
proportions, his moral, intellectual and physical
nature. This should be the end at which men of
all classes should aim, and it is this only which
constitutes real greatness. -Douglas Jerrold*

There's a reason that we look back on an-
cient times with envy. Back then men were
able to prove themselves and relished in the
battle to do so, conquering themselves a little more
each day. The modern era has its battles, but for
most, they aren't nearly enough to satisfy. We have
to put ourselves through the wringer if we want to
develop; to evolve.

There's no magic trick or sleight of hand. It's
a formula: Pain + Time = Growth. Go through the
pain, withstand it over time, and become stronger.
The problem is that most of us can live virtually

pain-free. Our lives are baby-proofed and climate-controlled.

To grow stronger, to reach your potential, you must be willing to put yourself through the pains that modern life has all but eliminated. Growth never comes without sacrifice. And it is to that sacrifice that we are called. Not one time, but every day, every moment. I won't pretend like I always succeed, but I do feel it. I feel the pull toward pain. That may sound masochistic, and maybe it is, but it is the way. It is the way because the destination we seek can only be reached by going through the fire.

We are called, and it is a strange calling. It is spiritual, intellectual and visceral at the same time. We are called to develop each of these areas, to get stronger in each of them, to become *more.* With each step, we realize that the next will be more difficult to take, but the rewards are promising, and so we do it. We don't engage in painful acts just for the hell of it. No, we bring pain upon ourselves in any number of ways because it is the only way to reach the fully evolved and balanced nature of the superior man.

We are called to reach for the heights and to obtain them, to make them ours. Of course each man's ultimate goal is different and varying in difficulty to achieve, but even so, the heights await us, the mountains beckon.

In days gone by men understood this path, and knew what was required of them. Most still weren't strong enough, but many were. These men of old conquered their world.

The burden, the mantle, has been passed down. Many have put it down, refusing the challenge. Most have done this. But there are still sparks of raw masculine energy, shining brightly in the world. There are men, some of which I call myself very fortunate to know, who refuse to accept the shit peddled by the mainstream and instead, daily, they choose to answer the call. No excuses, no lies, just authentic masculine power being directed in their lives, by them, to an ever net-positive outcome. It truly is something to behold.

Each of us men has this calling in our souls, to answer the call to authenticity in every area of our lives. Too few answer it.

I hope this book changes that.

I hope that more men begin to see the benefits of evolving mentally, physically and spiritually. Improving these three areas should be the focus of every man hoping to make a real, lasting, positive change in their lives and the lives of those around them. These three make up the trident of masculinity. To be well developed in these areas means that you are a man other people want to listen to and learn from.

It means that you are on the right path, that you are satisfied with yourself and your life. It means that you are right with God and that you are spiritually satisfied. It is the most worthy of goals and the only way to true self-actualization.

How do you achieve these things? With pain

and simplicity. I mean it when I say that pain is a necessary piece of the puzzle. Physical evolution does not happen in comfort unless we're talking about the slow evolution toward obesity. Physical strength is gained through physical exertion, period. That means you have to push yourself, push your body, tear it apart so that it can be rebuilt stronger, faster, better. You don't have to be the strongest or fastest or best, but you do have to have more good days than bad - meaning you must strive to better than you were yesterday. You don't need a bunch of equipment if you can't afford it, either. Just start somewhere. If you need the next step after this book, pick up Hunter Drew's 31 Days to Masculinity.

Men who can't *do,* pretend. Unable to slay the dragons in their own lives, they turn to kill them on screen. They waste so much time and energy on things that do nothing to develop them. There is an endless supply of entertainment to drown in, and the proliferation of entertainment and the acceptance of it as a viable means to pass all the hours in the day has made it extremely easy for men to pretend that they are dragon slayers when really they are remote-controllers of a digital manifestation of who they wish they were.

They are not serving the greater purpose of answering the call toward greatness in their own lives. They are doing the opposite of serving that purpose, the opposite of developing their mental capacities. It is as simple as a change in behavior, though, to fix this. Put down the remote and pick up a book. Find smart people to talk to, to learn from. Ask questions and then actually search for the answer. Just start by sitting quietly in a room alone for an hour, like in the last chapters *The Work*. Can you do it?

The point is that development of self and the ability to get over the self-loathing that so many men feel comes when you invest in yourself. You don't have to forgo entertainment completely, but you do need to take a hard look at where your hours are going and reallocate some of them, if not most of them, toward the betterment and stimulation of your mental capabilities. Just read a damn book. That act alone increases mental efficiency. Check out the list of some of the books that I think are awesome in the appendix at the end of this book.

Spiritually? Well, that's my favorite area to work on developing. In many cases, you grow spiritually as a result of working on your body and mind, by denying temptation and living a disciplined life. However, beyond that is talking to

God and listening for His still, small voice to answer you back. Look beyond the surface, the practical, the pragmatic. Delve into the depths of your soul and discover the majesty that lives there. You were created for more; to do more; to *be* more. Our spirits call out for something beyond the normal, the average, and that *Something* calls back.

Man must have meaning if he is to live up to all that his soul calls him toward, he must have a *why* and a *how.* I hope that I'm doing a decent job of articulating the state of things and the reason why it needs to change, but the how will be a bit different for each of us. What is it that you find meaning in? What excites your soul and brings genuine, unadulterated joy to your life?

If you don't know the answer to that then take my advice, get quiet and still and think about it without distraction. Listen to God, listen to your heart and discover what it is that you must do, what you are called to do.

The Work

You'll notice that I mentioned getting quiet and still again. That's because it's important! How was your hour alone? Did you come to any realizations? Were you able to do it?

How many times did you check your phone?

If you were able to do it then congratulations, you're in the minority. If not, you've got more work to do.

Did the *meaning* of your life come into question at all? Whether you made it the hour or not, did you think about your purpose?

You see, too many men go through life without ever finding their mission. It's sad to see so much wasted potential. I've seen a lot of it and you probably have too. Undoubtedly in yourself as well as in many men in your life. Why, though? Why must there be so much waste? So much aimless wandering?

Yes, not all who wander are lost, but most are. That's what needs to change. You must find your mission and begin living it out. Hopefully, you got some ideas about that when you spent an hour alone, in peace and quiet, but if you didn't then just do it again.

Take this one step at a time. Don't rush, but do *act.* I wasn't sure what my mission was at first. I had to figure it out by trial and error. It turned out that what I loved doing all along was what I should have been doing. Writing. That's my job. I'm a police officer too, but I feel like writing is my first job even though it hasn't paid nearly as well heretofore.

I love being a cop, but I love writing a lot more. I'm fortunate enough to be able to do two things I enjoy. What are you doing that you enjoy? My guess is "not much."

Change that. Start figuring out what it is that you love to do and do it. If you can make money off of it, figure out how to do that too. For instance, I love the art of writing itself, but I won't make a living off of writing books. I have to be a savvy marketer and editor as well. I have to have my finger on the pulse of the indie publishing industry. I have to study and learn and spend time honing my craft.

Whatever your mission is, it is going to take a lot of time. You will lose sleep. You will get stressed out over it. Remember when I said that I feel like writing is my first job? That's true, because I love it so much, and I'm working toward making a real income off of it, but I don't ever feel like I'm working when I'm writing, and that is a beautiful thing.

What do you love doing that maybe you've been neglecting because of whatever excuse you could come up with?

What is your mission?

What steps can you take to start living it out?

Figure it out. Write it down.

CHAPTER 6.5

"Dude, duck! Seriously! Get down!" Mike was whispering at the top of his voice.

"What? Why?"

"What the fuck do you think? Look who's here!" he said, pointing through the large windows into the gas station they were parked in front of.

The boy looked in that direction, seeing three figures decked out in red looking around inside.

"Oh fuck!" the boy's eyes went wide and he dropped into the floorboard of the van they were in.

"I fucking told you!"

"Oh shut the hell up. Thanks," the boy replied. "Shit! I wasn't expecting to see them. Do you see Rachel? Is she coming out? They better not fuck with her!"

"What are you going to do, fight them all? Then have their whole gang after you? Not a good fucking idea dude," explained Mike. He peeked up, watching the thugs in the store. "Maybe I should just go talk to them, let them know that I'll pay them back as soon as I can."

"That is a terrible idea. Don't you remember what they said they'd do to you if they saw you around and you didn't have their money?" Mike asked, eyes narrowed.

"Yeah, I fucking remember." The boy sat back, thinking how stupid he was for getting involved with the red-clad assholes. They had dumbass names too, he thought.

"Rachel is heading back out now. It doesn't look like they bothered her..." Mike trailed off.

"What?" asked the boy. "What's going on?" He sat back up, trying to keep his face hidden from the fluorescent lighting outside while still seeing through the windshield. He shook his head, berating himself for borrowing money from them.

The thugs followed Rachel out of the store. His eyes went wide as they started whistling at her. "Hey, Mami, where you goin'?" one of them said, Kirby was his name. He was fat and stupid but always carried a gun.

Rachel took the last couple of steps quickly, and as she opened her door she simply said, "Away from here."

"Nah, I don't think so," said another one, reaching for the door handle. She quickly jumped in and slammed the door just as Mike hit the lock button. "Go, sis, now."

The one by Rachel's door hit the window with open palms, anger plain on his face. "Back the fuck up!" the boy yelled at the three morons outside the van. Rachel took it as her cue to do the same. The van was still running so she threw it in reverse and slammed her foot down on the gas pedal. The van lurched backward, away from the now furious gangsters. They threw their arms up, making signs at the trio as if they didn't already know they were.

Luckily Rachel had nothing to do with people like them, so they'd be safe at her house. The boy sat back up in the seat, livid at himself and the gangsters.

"I'm really close to doing some shit that's going to put me away," he said aloud, red-faced. He'd always been like that, always extremely aware of the consequences of his actions. Sometimes, though, his anger got the better of him.

"Don't worry about them," said Rachel. "Once you give them back the money you owe them you never have to deal with them again."

Yeah, he thought, I don't see it going like that.

CHAPTER 7

"None of us will ever accomplish anything excellent or commanding except when he listens to this whisper which is heard by him alone. -Ralph Waldo Emerson

A poison requires an antidote. Fortunately, the poison of toxic masculinity has one. Good news for the feminized, the lazy, those unable to exhibit self-control, the cowards, and all those like them. The antidote is simple, when you think about it, but not easy. What about this path is easy? And is it not true that it's the most difficult things that bring about the most reward? We can leave the easy things for the surface dwellers and take on the real challenges for ourselves.

Simply put, the antidote is authenticity. Toxicity, with relation to masculinity, is nothing more than an inauthentic masculine nature. It's the masculine nature that is treated poorly; left by the wayside; improperly expressed. When the things spoken of in previous chapters are a reality, you have toxic masculinity. When boys and men bottle up or reject their masculine natures, or are otherwise unable to express it, negative shit is the result.

It's at this point that many a white knight will call for the outright abandonment of masculine virtues. They'll tell you that masculinity itself is the problem; that seeking improvement is offensive; that not everyone can meet our standards so we should lower them. To them, if someone isn't strong enough to compete, then it's the strength that is the problem, or the competition, but never their own weakness.

To men, weakness is detestable. I know full well that we all have strengths and weaknesses, but we understand that it's the weakness that needs to change. We need to work on our weaknesses, not belittle our strengths, to reach the heights we dream of. Likewise, the traits borne of repressed masculinity are the problem, not masculinity itself.

This is the way of this death cult that has been steadily building their power these many decades. They subvert everything good and true. Truth is offensive, there is no other god before the *self*, hard work is useless, tradition is evil, etc... They are cockroaches that scurry to the cracks in the walls when the light is turned on. The masculine spirit *is* that light, or possibly *a*light among several. Either way, they hate it. They hate it when the light shines in their darkness because it illuminates all that they are. You can lie to yourself all day long about how handsome you are at night, but when the sun comes up there is no denying what you really look like.

Masculinity is the light, the warmth, the strong, the *yang. It is the lights very nature to shine!* And shine you shall, you men of turbulence, of savagery, of honor and strength! You men of barbaric nobility! You are the antidote to a poisoned world; to a world in need of a touch of *wildness.* These house cats need to see what it means to be a lion, a beast in the wilderness. You must make them see things that will be imprinted on their eyelids when they close them at night. The truth is that seeing a man living right, living authentically, that is a sight that can't be unseen. You can't forget it, can't ignore it, and can't help but wish you dared to live that way yourself.

Masculine men must continue to stand our ground. We must not buckle under the weight of expectation. To reverse the effects of the poison that has been allowed to seep through the veins of our world, we must be the antidote. We must be the ship that braves the storm, the mountain upon which the storm brakes, the beast of noble savagery that ready and willing to deploy our weapons should the situation call for it.

You might be asking something along the lines of "How do I become an authentically masculine man." A common theme throughout this book has been to *follow your heart.* It's been worded various ways, but ultimately you must follow that voice inside of you, the one that you alone hear. Refer back to the quote at the beginning of this chapter. Emerson said it all. If you don't care for Emerson much, take the words for the value they hold anyway because they are true. Men who hope to accomplish excellent things must listen to that voice within him, the voice that no one but he hears.

I can't tell you about your mission in life. What I can do for you is encourage you, tell you that the feeling inside that something just isn't right isn't felt by you alone. I can give you principles that you can apply to your life to see it improve. We've gone over some of those already. Simply: exercise regularly, always be learning, spend time with God and with *meaning*.

Those three things, developing this trident of masculinity, body, mind, and spirit, can be further broken down. You can focus your physical training in things like lifting weights, calisthenics, long-distance running, mountain biking, crossfit, parkour, etc. Train your mind by learning, attend classes, seminars, webinars, subscribe to value producing email lists, ask questions, read...everything. As for developing yourself spiritually, I recommend spending time quietly, alone. Do the things that make you feel joy, get into nature, enjoy the peace of silence, ask questions of God and listen for the answers, meditate...

This isn't a how-to manual, but these are practical examples of things that you can begin to implement in your daily life that absolutely will shift your mindset, attitude, and trajectory in life. These things will help you to become the most authentic version of yourself. That authenticity is what is needed in this world of masks and lies and ignobility. Think of yourself as a gardener and everything you do toward developing yourself is another drop of water given to the plant of authenticity that you are cultivating within yourself.

It takes time. You will fail. I fail more than I succeed. It is the way of things. What's important is that you get up every single time you fall, no matter how much it hurts. Build your calluses and walk the fuck on. We have been involuntarily *civilized* to the point of the devastation of the masculine soul. It's time for a renaissance.

The Work

Be honest about your weaknesses. I know it isn't easy, not at first, to admit your foibles, your deficiencies, your Schwächen. But once more, you must. You cannot fix what you refuse to admit or accept.

Take out your list from Chapter 1 and spend time reviewing it, accepting every shortcoming that you listed. Don't make excuses for these qualities, whatever they may be, just accept them internally.

These are things that you've listed about yourself that you think you need to change. Is it your weight? Your work ethic? Your inattention to the family? Your irresponsibility? Your lack of education? Your desire to do something more than what you're currently doing?

It could be any of these, all of these, or things completely different. Think about what you've listed, and add more to the list. Add at least one more thing, if not several.

Chances are in Chapter 1 you held back. Now you've made a little progress. You've accepted that maybe you're not where you want to be in life. If you aren't already fairly fit then that one hour of working out hurt, but you did it. You have spent time in silence, listening only to the voice inside. You have stopped allowing others to dictate your path for you. When you feel you have something to say, you say it now, or at least you did once so far, which is a start. You've begun to figure out your mission in life.

Whatever timeline you're working on, I'd bet that you've changed, at least a little. Hopefully, you're more willing to be honest with yourself about where you stand in relation to where you *want* to be. So, as I said, add at least one more thing to your list.

Spend as much or as little time as you need to accept and internalize that these things are a part of you. This isn't an exercise meant to make you feel bad about yourself. What this should do is show you *exactly where you stand* and give you a pretty accurate idea of how hard you'll have to work to achieve your goals.

It's about becoming an integrated man. A man who doesn't lie to himself so that he can temporarily feel better about his worthlessness.

Read over the list from Chapter 1, add *at least* one more quality, habit, etc. about yourself that needs to change, and accept and internalize everything that is on the list as being part of you.

The good news is, as I've said before, people change. You can become more than you've been and succeed where you've failed. Hell, you already are doing those things, just keep at it.

CHAPTER 7.5

"Hey bro, we gotta go back to the restaurant," said Mike.

"What? Why?" the boy asked.

"Because I just realized they want me to start next Monday, but I have court so I can't," he said.

"Ah damn. Okay, I'll turn around," replied the boy.

"I guess I'll be starting on my own, then," said Felicity.

"Yeah, sorry," Mike said to her.

"It's okay, I was destined to be better than you at it anyway," she said, smiling.

That smile had sucked the boy in from the beginning; that and everything else about her. They'd been dating for a few months and he could not get enough of her. She was absolutely gorgeous, inside and out.

The boy looked over at her, smiling, "You are so beautiful."

She blushed, "Stop it." Her smile was unbelievably beautiful.

They pulled into the restaurant, doing a circle around the building before parking.

"Oh shit man, why does this always happen?"

asked Chrissy.

"What?" the boy asked, looking back at her.

"Douchebag and the fat bitch are here," she said simply. She'd always had a bit of attitude and it came out most often when she saw people she hated.

Mike just said, "Ah, it'll be fine," as he got out of the car and started walking toward the restaurant.

The boy just so happened to hate the douchebag too. "Hey, let's stay in the car while he goes in, babe. I don't want you to get into a fight."

Just then the boy looked through the rear view mirror to see the douchebag spit through his car window into Mike's face as he walked by his car. There was to be no waiting. The boy jumped out of the driver's seat of the car and made a beeline for the one from which the saliva had flown. Mike had wiped the spit off and kept walking, but the boy wasn't above beating the shit out of the douche bag, and that is what he did.

He reached the passenger side of the car and the first thing he noticed was that the bag must have been confident, given that he was still wearing his seatbelt, and still had the seatbelt down. He even went so far as to spit on the boy when he walked up. He must have thought that the boy wouldn't fuck with him. He was wrong. The boy hated being spit on so much that he completely let go of his rage.

With his left hand, the boy grabbed the door frame and put his left knee into the door so that the bag couldn't escape. He then began beating the douchebag senseless through his open car window. The bag through a punch which landed squarely on the boy's nose, blood spurted down his face and onto his jacket, but he didn't care. All he wanted was to kill this fucking douchebag.

He laughed inside as the douchebag tried to climb through the window with his seatbelt still on, trying to escape the rain of blows to his face and head. He kept swinging again and again until his arm hurt from exertion, then kept striking in spite of the pain. The douchebag tried to unbuckle his seatbelt but to no avail. This entire time Felicity had been trying to pull the boy away from the car, trying to get him to stop hitting the douchebag, but he wouldn't be deterred.

Eventually, though how long it had been the boy had no idea, people started to gather around the beating. At some point, the boy's hood had been ripped off of his jacket, and blood still flowed from his nose. He stopped hitting the bag and stepped back, letting him out of the car. The douchebag got out slowly and appeared dazed, face swollen.

"You shouldn't have fucking done that," said the boy, feeling the anger subside. He heard the word "cops" and decided it was a good time to leave. He grabbed Felicity's hand and stormed back to the car. Little did the boy know then, but this was not the end.

CHAPTER 8

An acorn is not an oak when it is sprouted. It must go through long summers and fierce winters and endure all that frost, and snow, and thunder, and storms, and side-striking winds can bring before it is a full-grown oak. So a man is not a man when he is created; he is only begun. His manhood must come with years. He who goes through life prosperous, and comes to his grave without a wrinkle, is not half a man. Difficulties are God's errands and trainers, and only through them can one come to the fullness of manhood. -Henry Ward Beecher

L et's take it back for a bit. As a young boy, I was in love with maps. I just really enjoyed looking at them. They told of a whole wide world just waiting for me to explore, ripe with adventure and dangerous obstacles for me to overcome. I wanted to climb and search and hunt and find. Maps, to me, were a gateway to stories untold.

When I was a bit older I grew to love fantasy books and especially the maps that they sometimes had at the beginning or spread throughout the text. They taught me that there was far more to explore than just this one planet. I learned that "out there," somewhere, was my place in the universe. A place with dragons and magic and danger and power and women. My imagination went wild with the thoughts of heroes and villains and battle.

I learned that the universe is a *huge* place, to put it mildly and that the exploration of it would never be complete. Even if the books I read were fiction, and the thoughts I thought were just thoughts, I knew somewhere deep inside that there was magic in this universe and that I wanted it to be mine.

The problem was, no one I knew shared my enthusiasm. Not only did no one share my enthusiasm, but no one even bothered to mention the fantasy of it all. Don't get me wrong, I still love fantasy novels, but to the "me" of my childhood, they were real. I know better now (at least I think I do) but it was a hard won bit of knowledge. It was painful, extremely, to grow to learn that this world is limited and fantastical magic isn't real like was depicted in the stories I read.

I think that one of the most painful parts of it all was that, as I said above, no one mentioned it. I wish someone had thought to guide me into understanding the reality of it all, but I had to find that wall by flying into it at top speed. To be honest, it broke my heart.

It's because I put my faith in the wrong map. I didn't have the map that would lead me to manhood, I had the maps that would lead me to perpetual adolescence. I don't think there is anything wrong with those maps or those books, but left alone, with no real concept of just how different the real world is from those imaginary ones, they brought pain.

Of course, I don't blame the maps, that would be silly, but I do blame the men in my life at the time. I don't begrudge them anything. They are forgiven and out of my life. However, I can see where the shortcomings were.

I wasn't given a map to manhood. I didn't understand all that it took to become a man and no one taught me, in large part because the men in my life were themselves stuck in their own extended adolescence, one that they are still stuck into this day as far as I know. It has ruined them and they refuse to change.

That's fine. That's their choice. But there are many men today, likewise misinformed about the truth, who are seeking that authentic masculinity. They want to experience true strength, purpose, and clarity. They want to fully understand and be able to grasp their mission(s) in life. But they don't have the map to lead them to their destination.

Most times it's our father's influence, or the lack thereof, that sets the stage for us. An overbearing or under-present father can break us. The power that fathers wield in the lives of the children is most often second to none, yet most don't even realize it. Fathers define their children and the children are too impressionable to stop it.

It wasn't until I was a grown man that I realized that there was a path out of the life molded by those who raised me. I fumbled around for so long, trying to find the way on my own. I had no idea where to start or where to look, but I knew that there had to be more than was passed down to me. There had to be a way to navigate all of the traps that were laid out before me. How could I, a man, a husband, and a father, make better headway?

Honestly, the road was so difficult that many times I just quit. I stopped all forward progress and went back to eating shit food and allowing myself to drown in video games and television. That may not sound like that bad of a life, but inside my soul was crying out for the truth. I just *knew* that I was meant for more; that God was calling me to more. The not-so-funny thing is that the voice inside is quiet. It isn't demanding, or at least I didn't experience it that way. I still don't experience it that way. I hear it when the hustle and bustle calms, when my family is asleep or when I'm driving alone. I hear it when I don't drown it out.

Thankfully, it's persistent. Never has that voice, the one calling me on toward the fullness of my existence, disappeared. Every time I stop for a moment, I hear it. It tells me that I am called toward things greater than the average of modernity. Things that involve following the calling of my soul. It's a calling that urges me off of the beaten path, off of the boardwalk, into the caves and the waters and the mountains and the wilderness.

I will not be a man who died without living, but to fulfill that commitment I must actually *live.* It isn't easy and it requires courage, but following the calling of one's soul is the only way to live *fulfilled!* The discerning man will see that I'm talking about neglecting the way the world would have you live, the way your friends, family, co-workers, and others live. He will see that most neglect their own souls and that he must neglect *them* to some extent, or to the full extent if he is going to live a life he can be proud of.

He must make judgments about others and the choices they make and the paths they choose to follow, and he must willfully choose to take his own path, regardless of whether others like it or not. He must live authentically.

The Work

Separate the wheat from the chaff, and throw the chaff in the fire.

Not everyone has your best interests in mind. In fact, you are probably the only one that does. Which connections in your life are fruitless? Which ones bring you down?

Remove them.

You mustn't spend time with or around people who are bad for your progress. Think about all those people that bring nothing and the ones that actively bring discord, and cut them off.

Don't pretend to be friends with them, don't lie about how you feel toward them. Go back to Chapter 2 and do that work again. If you must, tell them to their faces that you've got bigger plans for your life and don't have time to waste on futile, unnecessary relationships.

Tell them you don't like them, or that they are bad for your forward momentum. You don't have to be a dick about it, but you do have to be honest. No lying allowed.

Feel free to, as they say, *nope the fuck out.*

This is another difficult step to take, but more friends can be made. Friends with the right type of mindset await those whose time isn't constantly consumed by people stuck in a never ending loop of

Jon Parker

drunken weekends or video game filled evenings.

Get away before their poison infects you. You are on the right path and it's leading to a better you. Ultimately, you are going to set the bar in your life and surroundings and most people won't be able to come close to reaching it. That's okay, not everyone has what it takes.

But you do. After all, you're reading this book, doing the work, and you've committed to bringing about the best in your life. Others get offended when it's even suggested that they need to improve. Those won't change until life drops a massive shit sandwich on their plate and they're forced to eat it. Hell, they may not even change then.

However, what they do is unimportant, because they no longer have any power in your life. Hear me when I say this: it doesn't matter who it is, if they are bad for your life then they have to go. At the very least you have to disallow them to have any say in what you do in your life. Maybe they'll see the bar rising and jump on before it's too late, maybe not. Either way, that decision is up to them.

Your life is up to *you*. Focus on what is yours. Removing the negative influences from your life will compound your effectiveness and astoundingly increase forward momentum. It may be lonely for a while, but that just means there's more time to focus on growth.

Remove the negative influences from your life. *Do not* waste time on people that don't care about you, or that don't care about themselves.

CHAPTER 8.5

"I'm so happy we finally got away from there," said Felicity.

The boy smiled, running his fingers through his hair with one hand, taking a drag with the other. "Me too babe. We can do better for ourselves where we're going than we could out here."

"You sure you're going to like the desert? It's a lot different than this humidity," she said.

"Ah I'm sure it'll be fine," he said, flicking his cigarette away. He reached around her, pulling her into a hug, lifting her off the ground and spinning her in a circle.

"Putmedownputmedownputmedown!!" she said, laughing and smacking him lightly. He laughed, happier than he could ever remember being.

They were in Amarillo, Texas. The air around the Greyhound bus station smelled...weird. The boy couldn't put his finger on it. Maybe...engine oil and meth? He sat her down and kissed her once on the lips.

"I love you," he said, watching her beautiful blue eyes sparkle in the afternoon sun.

"I love you too baby," she said, squeezing him tight.

They were going on an adventure, nearly 2000

miles from where he'd lived all his life, to an area packed with millions of people, to make a life for themselves. They'd moved in with the boy's uncle for three months to work and save up enough money to get bus tickets out of the Midwest and into a new life. They'd had enough of the path they'd been headed down, and at 17 years old they were going to get married and start a life together.

People of seemingly every race, color and creed milled about the bus station, inside and outside. A red cobblestone road stretched from between two streets, creating the pathway by which the buses could arrive and depart. Up to this point, the ride had been interesting, to say the least, and he was sure that it would continue to prove to be that.

The boy had truly never been happier before. He and his girl were leaving, finally. There was nothing left for them in the place that they'd departed, and their whole lives lay before them. The boy, still not yet a man, turned at the sound of squeaking bus brakes.

"I think that's our ride babe," he said, grabbing their bags.

She took a deep breath. "Onward and upward," she said, smiling.

CHAPTER 9

*"As iron sharpens iron, so one man sharp-
ens another." (Proverbs 27:17)*

When I was going at this alone, without guidance, I had made some progress on my own, but everything gained felt earned by crawling through broken glass. I had reached a point where I was in a perpetual cycle of starting and giving up and starting and giving up, etc. Eventually, tired of it all, I took on a "fuck the world and everyone in it" attitude. This is one extreme that many men take. With the world so seemingly cold, we turn our backs and shun the ways of it. Thankfully, it was not long after this, when the nihilism had yet to fully mature, I began to encounter some of those like-minded men.

Hunter Drew was the first man I ever came across that was seeking to help other men reclaim their authentic masculine natures. The things he said connected on a deep level and soon enough I found myself committed to the first ever *31 Days to Masculinity* program, called "Men of March."

For the first time in my life, I was in step with other men on a shared mission. For the first, I knew what brotherhood felt like. And that is the key, isn't it? It's that brotherhood, the camaraderie, which helps men to *become* men.

Each man's first mentor should be his father. Many of us lacked that mentor-ship. Many of us lacked a father. Many of us had a father, or some semblance of one, who just didn't give a shit. Fathers are so often just absent or unwilling or both, and it is insane.

Gone, in large part, are the days of elder men giving young men rites of passage. And so too has gone true battle, true hunting for survival, true tests of strength and skill.

Fortunately, we have our brothers. And as Jack Donovan said in *The Way of Men*, "...honor requires accountability to other men." The ideals of the tribe are being revived all across the West and that is a good thing. Men have stepped up to test themselves and to challenge their comrades in the widespread absence of true, honorable masculinity.

They've done so, we've done so, to keep that fire burning. Manhood is largely defined by how we individually relate to other men. When we surround ourselves with men who are taking control of their lives, who are keeping their word, maintaining self-discipline, consistently pushing the boundaries, and leading with strength and humility, then we can each grow to that point and in turn, serve as an example for other men.

To the men who are lost, finding like-minded men who can serve as your brothers and rivals will have a greater effect in your life than I can adequately describe here. For me, that came first in 31DtM and then in the form of the *Fraternity of Excellence.*

This group essentially formed from what was once simply a desire in the hearts of men. Craig James and Hunter Drew saw the gap, they saw the men falling into it, and decided to act. Now we are a Brotherhood of Exceptional Men, striving every day to be more than we were the day before; to be stronger leaders, better husbands, and fathers, more powerful in word and will, more intentional in the everything we do, and to be more physically, mentally and spiritually fit.

These are men that look into the fire and walk forward, allowing themselves to be refined by the heat therein. We don't accept excuses and we don't lie to ourselves. We each uphold our own noble code, as well as that of the *Iron Brotherhood.*

My life has changed drastically since I learned that I could learn from other men; since I learned that other men were experiencing the same thing I experienced. There are a lot of men that would benefit from joining our ranks. If that sounds like you then I implore you to give it a go. I wouldn't be behind it or a part of it if I didn't wholeheartedly believe in those men and in the growth that has come from us banding together in our shared mission. It is not for everyone, I can promise that. It takes grit, self-discipline, a strong will and a willingness to change in order to make it as an Iron Brother, but it is doable for those who want it.

Whether you decide to give it a go or not, remember that it takes men to build up men. If you are seeking growth and achievement, a mission oriented mindset with the ability to lead yourself to where you want to be in life, then it is helpful to have other men help to draw the map. You may haphazardly make some positive gains, like I did, by trudging blindly forward, but having that map in hand will help you avoid pitfalls and save time on your journey.

Think about these things in the coming days and honestly reflect on who you are as a man, where you currently stand and the areas in your life that need further development. How could you benefit from a brotherhood? Personally, I'm stronger than I've ever been in every area of my life. I'm not joking when I say that. I understand the weight behind those words, but it is true.

Never in my life have I felt this level of strength, purpose, and clarity. Things that I thought were impossible are now a reality because of my willingness to learn from other men, and that is powerful.

You see, we often get caught up in our ways, refusing to budge. I've been called stubborn and bull-headed plenty of times in my life, and it was this obstinate attitude that played a major role in stunting my growth as a man. I wanted to become a real man, to become stronger, more capable, worthy of honor; but I refused to listen to the advice of those who knew better than me. I *actually* refused to believe that anyone knew better than me at all, let alone listen to their advice.

One of the most difficult lessons to learn was that I don't know anywhere near as much as I had once believed. It is humbling to see other men surpass you while you sit by on the sidelines, red-faced, refusing to play the game because you think the rules are stupid.

So much has changed for me and my family as a direct result of learning this lesson though, and it would be remiss of me to write this book and not drive home this point: *listen.* Every chance you get, listen to men around you. Let yourself learn from their experiences, both good and bad. Soak up as much experience-by-association as you are able because it is the foolish man who learns only by his own failures. While our failures teach invaluable lessons, if you can learn from those of others then you will always be one step ahead in life.

Brotherhood is so important to cultivating genuine masculinity. Seek those men who would build you up rather than those who would tear you down, and be wary because some will tear you down all the while having no ill intent toward you.

You must always be on guard and you must continually evaluate yourself and your decisions to make sure you are headed in the right direction. It may sound difficult to you, and it is, but the rewards far outweigh the pain.

The Work

Seek a brother and find one. If you've got a best friend or brother that is always trying to get you to do better for yourself, listen to them. Masculinity can only be conferred and confirmed by other men, not by you alone and not by women. If you don't then do whatever you've got to do to find one. You don't have to already know them, but you do have to ask them for help. A brother is born for adversity and the road is far more traversable if you have a brother to walk it with.

"A friend loves at all times, and a brother is born for adversity."
-Proverbs 17:17

Fools refuse to listen to the advice of those who have gone before. Get out of your ego and listen to what they have to say. If you don't have a friend or a brother or anyone in your life that can help you here, like I didn't, then go out and meet people. Go to the gym, for instance. Hell, go online and check out FoE. Well over a hundred men from all different backgrounds and places in the world have found genuine brotherhood therein.

Ultimately it doesn't matter where you find positive influences, it just matters that you do. This part is just as important as *The Work* from Chapter 7.

Those holes left by the people you've cut from your life will just fill with more of the useless unless you proactively find useful people to fill them with.

Don't get me wrong, people aren't products and I don't mean to make it sound as if they are. I guess I just don't know any better way to say that some are duds and others are studs.

My brothers are successful, and working their asses off to be more so. They are the epitome of everything in this book and more. I count myself extremely fortunate to be both in The Fraternity of Excellence and a newer group called The Masculine Pulp Association, exclusively for masculine fiction authors. I was invited to MPA by an FoE brother, and a rising star in the indie publishing world, **Adam Lane Smith**. Since joining that group I've been continually held accountable and encouraged by the men there.

I can't say enough good things about being part of a brotherhood of men with like minds and goals. If that doesn't sound like you, I don't care. You still need to find another man or brotherhood of men that will keep you accountable.

That's the work for this chapter. **Find a man, or more than one, with whom you can swap notes. Forge a brotherhood and utilize it.**

CHAPTER 9.5

"2-1-9-6!"

"That's not how you count silly boy," she said.

"Mama?"

"Yes, baby boy?"

"2-1-9-6!!" the boy ran off, giggling his heart out.

She smiled warmly and turned to the boy, now becoming a man, slowly but surely.

"I'm going to remember this forever," he said to her, chuckling. "Someday, when he has kids of his own, I'm going to teach them to say '2-1-9-6' just to see if he remembers."

"He probably won't. He's so young still," she replied.

"Yeah, you're probably right. At the very least we'll remember, and I bet it'll make you smile someday to hear your grandchildren saying what our son says all the time." He laughed again.

He leaned forward over the railing, enjoying the early Phoenix morning. Dew covered the grass below the balcony of their second story apartment. The grass made him think of where he'd come from. He'd grown to love the desert, though, in a way that he'd never expected to.

The Valley was his home and he knew that no matter where they ended up, he'd never find another place quite like it. Many people couldn't handle the heat, the harshness, but he reveled in it. He looked south, thinking of Camelback Mountain.

It was his favorite place in the city. From its peak, somewhere in the neighborhood of 1,330 feet above ground level, one could see the entire Phoenix metropolitan area spread out in all directions, covering the land between the mountains. He loved to climb up there and just be. Too few enjoyed the state of simple existence, he thought. It seemed that lately, he was becoming ever more introspective; contemplative.

He was working in security and so had found himself with a lot of extra time to just think. One thing had become glaringly obvious: he had to make something more of his life, for both himself and his family. He had to do better for his children than was done for him. Not just better, though, but far better. He needed his children to know that it was possible to rise out of the worst circumstances. As one of his childhood heroes, William Thatcher said, "A man can change his stars." He needed his family to believe that it was possible in the same way that he believed it was. The only way to have them believe it was to show them it was possible.

He'd already committed to changing doing the thing, he just didn't know how. The surprises that would come his way would prove to be world shattering...

CHAPTER 10

*"This is the test of your manhood: How much is
there left in you after you have lost everything
outside of yourself?" -Orison Swett Marden*

T his book is turning out to be less cohesive
than I'd like, but so is my brain, I suppose... I
understand that about myself; that my brain
is all over the place. Over these last few years, I've
come to know myself quite well. It sounds strange,
saying that as if it is out of the ordinary. I mean,
don't people *know themselves?* I didn't know myself,
not really, for most of my life. It's a terrifying feeling, not knowing who you are.

I also discovered that this is way more common than I thought. People don't know themselves
today. Why? That's an easy one. I've talked about it
several times already. It's too easy to drown out the
noise with constant entertainment. Most people

can't sit in peace and quiet, reflecting on themselves. It's scary, trying to get to know yourself. I was scared at first. Learning more about me meant that I had to recognize and accept all of my shortcomings and failures, all the shitty things I've done and terrible thoughts I've thought. It's easy to mask it in anything and everything, to stifle the voice crying out inside. It's difficult to sit in silence and talk to God or talk to your own heart.

But a proper understanding of yourself is critical to being able to follow this path and surviving it, thriving on it. You must accept yourself for who you are if you want to be able to grow. So, start with that. Start by getting to know yourself. Do whatever it takes to accomplish this goal. Think about it for a bit and you'll come up with something. If you don't, just keep sitting in silence and thinking on it.

Once you have a decent understanding of who you are, you can then start putting your feelers out and try to understand a little of what is going on around you. With a realized sense of self, your perceptions and opinions will likely be different than before and you'll see that what you thought to be true about a great many things is not true. It's a strange and wonderful phenomenon.

Even if you already know yourself pretty well it can't hurt to spend some time honing in on your perceptions of yourself. How you see yourself affects virtually everything in your life, so it is important to have a firm grasp of it.

Do you see yourself as a good man? Or perhaps

you see a bad man when you look in the mirror? Or maybe just an unimportant one? Just those three options open up a hell of a lot of possibilities as far as how they may affect how you act in, and interact with, the world and its denizens. A good person wouldn't be an asshole for no reason, right? But maybe you are an asshole for no real reason sometimes. How do you reconcile those two things?

Would an unimportant man be loved by others? Maybe you are well-liked and everyone enjoys being around you. Doesn't that mean that you are important to those people? So how can you see yourself as unimportant if there is evidence to the contrary?

What of a bad person? Would they help an old lady load a 50lb bag of dog food in the back of her truck? Well, you're a bad person, right? Why'd you help her?

I know these are simplistic and not completely applicable, but you get the idea, right? There are so many more possible interpretations of perceptions that you may have about yourself that could be causing strain on your soul. You've got to be honest with yourself about who you are, good or bad, and work to change it if you think change is needed.

I'd bet that every single person who ever reads this book or any other book in history (so pretty much everyone) has some quality or qualities about themselves that they'd remove in a heartbeat if they could do so. Such is the way of man. We are imperfect, ever seeking perfection. The point to re-member is that you must have a good grasp on who you are, what you believe and how you see exist-ence. If you can do this then you are standing on solid rock with the minority of strong men.

We know well how lost men are today. We're lied to, promised that things will be better if we just sit down, shut up and listen.

What men don't understand is that those mak-ing these promises of a better tomorrow are sirens, singing us into the depths of the sea. They call us to our death, and what an inglorious death it is!

An understanding of who we are as men, what it means to really cultivate the masculine spirit of man, is necessary if we hope to keep our heads above water.

The Work

List time once more.

Write a list of every good quality that you possess. Don't hold back. Just like with the list of things about yourself that you'd like to change, the Schwächen, put it all out there. Everything you like about yourself needs to be on the list.

We're not all doom and gloom around here. Good things deserve to be lifted up and cultivated. So begin doing that. Write the list. This time we're not going to wait for you to look back on it and accept these things later.

Take all the time you need, and as much paper (actual or otherwise), as is necessary to get it all out. Gush on about it, seriously. Once you are finally done, read it, read it and re-read it; and *internalize it.* Understand that these things, in addition to the negative, are a part of you.

You wouldn't be who you are without both the good and bad. That's not to say that you want to keep the negative shit. That stuff is going to need to change. But everything about you has played a part in how you got to where you are.

CHAPTER 10.5

"A man can change his stars..."

The concept had been whirling around in his heart and mind for years. All he'd ever wanted to do was to change his stars, to change how his life should turn out according to society, given his upbringing and the extreme lack of advantages he'd been given. He had nothing, came from nothing. But an overwhelming desire existed in his heart to reach for stars that others said he'd never touch.

The desert whipped by as he drove along the lonely, two lane highway to where he did not know. He'd just needed to get away for awhile; to think. Huge mountains loomed in the distance in every direction, and the space between him and them was filled with saguaro cacti, desert ironwoods, chuparosas, velvet mesquites and any other number of plants adapted to the hot, dry desert climate of southern and central Arizona.

A single cloud floated overhead, he could see it through the open sun-roof, as he sped down the deso-

late road. He thought once more of his favorite childhood movie. He held the fictional character of William Thatcher in high regard. Not so the real version of the man whose name he assumed in the movie, though.

The real Ulrich Von Lichtenstein believed that it was a knight's greatest ambition to serve his lady and to earn a spot as her lover. He took it so far as to drink the water that she used to wash her hands, had facial surgery in a time when it could mean death and severed one of his fingers (twice) to prove that he was worthy of her affections. He nearly drowned himself because of her as well, being saved in time by a lying messenger. All this while having an actual wife at home.

No, the real man named Ulrich Von Lichtenstein was not a role model, but a chivalric loser of a man. However, his fictional counterpart, with sure shortcomings of his own, came from nothing and obtained everything he ever wanted.

He had dreams as well; dreams that he'd been told his entire life were not achievable by those like him. But it was bullshit, right? It had to be. Listening to others had never been one of his strengths, so he found it increasingly easy to disregard the negative opinion others held about his dreams and what he was doing and would do to make them a reality.

He'd watched too many people give up before they'd ever really even tried. He'd seen them turn down the wrong path, over and over again. He simply couldn't have that life, he refused to live it. He was reminded, then, of a quote from Abraham Lincoln in a letter to John Stuart in 1841: "To remain as I am is impossible; I *must die or be better, it appears to me."*

Certainly, his circumstances were different than those of Lincoln, but no truer words could he think of in that moment. To remain as he was would be suicide. He'd been down that road. It was overrated.

CHAPTER 11

"Where are you, creators? Noble beasts? Where are the men of the wheel and the chariot, the terrors of the steppe, the men of thunder and the shining sun? Where are the men who make marvels and masterpieces, who found orders and demand not merely utility - but beauty? - Jack Donovan, A More Complete Beast

You are stifled. You may not even realize it right now, but the society that surrounds you seeks to stifle you, suffocate you, and box you in. The rules they implement are walls designed to close in around you, crushing you and your spirit into oblivion. They create rules that they say are for safety, but what they do is sanitize you, keep you away from growth.

It starts in school with "Don't run in the halls," and "Don't run with scissors." "Stay inside the fence," they say. But what they don't understand is that we were made to go over the garden wall, out into the wilderness, and our hearts beat for the adventure of it. But that isn't what the death cult wants, is it? They want you to be a good boy, to sit down and shut up and do as you're told because according to them, you aren't needed anymore. They told you they didn't need you, if not in word than in deed, attitude, and lifestyle.

"You told them to sit down and shut up and that they were no longer needed; that men, real Men, were no longer needed, you said." - Roman McClay, Sanction I

They said that even the smallest bit of danger is too much. The germs will kill you and the fall will break you and the others won't like you if you don't do what you're told. When you became a man you kept to the rules because it's what you'd been trained to do for your entire life. You've asked for permission, skirted around conflict and kept your feet on the ground. Because grounded is good, right? Forget the fliers, the explorers, the wandering souls of the world. Your office is safe, your routine is safe, and your life is safe.

The rules become "Wear your seat belt" and "Don't drive too fast." They say "Don't leave the boardwalk." Ah, the boardwalk... The antithesis of man's wild nature. The inviolable boardwalk; the snug home of the pussyfooters of the world... More on this later...

So, what does an unnecessary man do? What is he to do with the voice inside that tells him he is meant for more than cubicles and climate control and sitting quietly in his chair? What do you do, you noble beast?

I think there is a more pertinent question to ask here, and that is, *Since when did you give a shit about what other people thought of you?* Let's leave worrying about that for the weak, those who depend on the approval of the burgeoning cadre of screeching harpies that seek to gain full control over the danger to them that is the masculine heart. Why is that approval important? Was it ever?

I remember seeking their approval. Many never did, and I applaud them. But for me, I didn't even realize there was another option. I've said it before and I'll say it again: I was a "chivalric loser." I put women, all women, on a pedestal because "Dammit! They're women!" The conditioning was strong and it took a long time before I was able to see what I was missing. There is a line in Roman McClay's book *Sanction,* which I think will fit here nicely.

> *"...by the time I left high school I had begun the process to no longer give a fuck what people far dumber, far less ethical, far less creative, far less loyal or romantic or alive in their hearts and balls, thought of me." -Roman McClay, Sanction I*

It wasn't by the time I left high school, but it happened. I stopped caring what people thought because I realized that most of them were, like the quote above says, dumber, less ethical, less creative, less loyal, less romantic or less alive in their hearts and balls. Why should such opinions concern me?

The answer is that they shouldn't. Those people's opinions are nothing but a bad joke. They've banned together under a flag of equality but in reality, they only care about equality up until you disagree with them on even the smallest points. They are children in the guise of adults, playing the part in a very poor fashion.

They despise honor, vigor, strength and the act of truly living. They crowd together because they have neither the fortitude nor the tenacity to stand alone to face the storm of life. They live without verdure, without vibrancy, without life. They are a society of masturbatory bonobos, a *verein* of those carrying the poor reflection of their better, greater relatives. They stay on the path beaten down for them by those many that have trod that way before.

You, though, Man, are different. You are called to fly like the peregrine falcon, the golden eagle... To hunt, to live, to revel in the joy of flight! You are the greater of the great apes, the fiercest of the beasts of the jungle. It is yours to live and die and to *truly do both.* Many men die long before they are buried because they don't take up the mantle of masculinity and live with it, growing, thriving, and strengthening themselves, surviving... In so refusing his divine mantle he finds that he *never really lived or died.* What can a man say of his existence that had a false life and a false death? One thing is for certain: he can count himself among the majority of modernity.

Man must do that which his heart calls him

to do, otherwise, he will lose it. "Don't give into your fears. If you do you won't be able to talk to your heart," says Coelho in *The Alchemist.* The loss of one's heart is death in this life, and this is what you see when you look at your surroundings, modern Man: death. The rules supposedly meant to promote safety in truth often promote the dying of the soul.

A small thing happened to me recently. It's funny to me how the smallest of actions can have the most profound effect on one's life. I found myself on a boardwalk, staring in awe at one of the most beautiful sites in nature that I had ever seen. People had built a cozy boardwalk leading down into an amazingly beautiful valley into which also poured a waterfall. At the bottom of the waterfall was an unforgettable bluish-green pool of water. Frondescence surrounded me, songbirds sang above and water continued to rush over the cliff's side.

It was here, standing on the edge of this boardwalk, that I found signs telling me to remain on it; to keep my feet off of the natural ground. This irked me almost instantaneously. Who were these people to tell me that I couldn't explore nature? Was this place too sacred for man to tread? I had a choice to make, then. Would I be the type of man who stays on the boardwalk, or would I be the Man that follows the calling in his heart? Nature was calling me to be a part of it, my soul longed to experience the intense, invigorating water; to walk where the tentative, the play-it-safers, dare not tread.

Jon Parker

Such a small thing... Yet it was mandatory for my heart to go on beating. Many have never experienced this. Most never will. It saddens me that they won't feel this ephemeral yet eternal feeling, this sublime, ineffable emprise isn't lived by everyone, everywhere. But that is the way of things, isn't it? Would such a thing be as memorable, as personal, as special, if it were a thing that *everyone* accomplished?

I wonder about that. And I wonder what will become of the world as it grows increasingly more docile, more domesticated. Those who would have become great warriors in centuries or millennia past are now declawed house cats. It pains me greatly to see this, because I've seen what *was,* and it was greater. It was *more human.*

So what do I say to you who seek a different way? Start by stepping, jumping, leaping from the boardwalk wholeheartedly and unapologetically. Roar like the lion and beat your chest like the gorilla, and find your way in the wilderness in spite of what the world has become. You who the world would civilize, you who they would shackle and chain - know that you were created to be a warrior, by a Warrior. In the image of God was man created, and God is no civilized gentleman, *but the very essence of life and glory and strength and courage!*

And if they call you "TOXIC" for being who you were created to be, then laugh and forge forward, for you know which of you is toxic, which of you brings death by *being dead*, and which of you is *alive!*

The Work

Do something that makes you feel alive.

Maybe that means leaving the boardwalk and venturing into the forbidden waters. Maybe that means skydiving. Maybe that means taking a nap in a mountain forest.

I don't know what it means for you, but I'm sure you can figure that out. This isn't just something that you haven't done before. I don't care if you've done this before. It just has to be something that makes you feel alive.

For me that most often means following the calling of my heart, regardless of boundaries imposed by others. It means going where I must go and experiencing what life has to offer and damn the consequences.

Go, leave the boardwalk, and find yourself in your heart's calling.

Men are dead or dying in large part and it hurts my heart to see it. It's like watching a unicorn die. The masculine spirit is something sacred, that shouldn't be allowed to die. It's the same for the feminine spirit. These are the basis of *who we are* as humans.

I feel like holy ground is being trampled underfoot of this death cult that seems to be running the social show in the West. It's disgusting and I will do everything I can to stop it from happening. As should you. So go and do something that makes you feel alive. Stoke the fires of your masculine spirit and burn away the darkness that threatens to envelop you.

Tell your heart to beat again; make it beat again; give it a reason to beat again!

CHAPTER 11.5

"Honestly, I don't know who I am," he said.

"What do you mean," asked the male half of the suicide prevention team.

"I mean there is a huge rift between who I should be, the way I was raised, and who I want to be, and I'm lost somewhere in the middle."

"Well, how were you raised?" asked the woman.

He laughed, "That's an interesting story..." He looked up at her. She was watching him patiently but expectantly.

"The short version?" he asked, then continued without waiting for an answer. "My parents were violent and abusive. They were addicted to alcohol, weed, meth, etc. They taught me how to drink and how to smoke weed. We were always having to move because neither of them could hold a job and any money that did come in swiftly went toward their habits. If it weren't for food stamps I honestly don't know what we'd have eaten. My sister ran away to live with our grandparents at 15. I left home and was homeless at 15..." he trailed off, old memories surfacing. "I remember when I was about 12 or 13 years old, we lived in this old shitty

trailer in the country with no heat or water. My mother thanked me for not complaining. Even though I was angry, it made me feel strong..."

"Look, I've always had anxiety and depression. I've always been hyperactive. I've always, always, been angry. I think extremely dark thoughts, often. I know that I've got issues. I just want to be able to control myself; my emotions," he said. "I can't handle this incessant pain."

"Have you thought about seeing a counselor of some kind?" the guy asked.

"I have, but I don't have the money to do that. I don't have insurance, either. I'm kind of stuck right now..."

"You know, I think you should do some research on 'mindfulness'," said the woman.

"What's that," he said, looking her in the eyes.

"It's kind of like meditation. It is focusing on the present moment, the here and now, exclusively, for a few minutes at a time. I think that could help you get out of your head and into the moment a little bit. Without a way to see a specialist that's all the advice I have," she said. She looked like she wanted to say more but just didn't have the words.

"I've noticed something about you these past few minutes. Well, this whole conversation, really. You seem to be very self-aware. It looks like you understand what's going on inside of you. Keep paying attention to that. This is just my opinion but it seems that this awareness has helped you get through some tough times," the guy said.

He grew contemplative. Maybe the guy was right. He had always been quite aware of his internal state... Maybe knowing what was happening had been the thing that kept him from pulling the trigger...

"Thanks for coming all this way," he said a few moments. "I'll look into what you said."

They all shook hands and the suicide prevention team left. He had a lot of thinking to do...

CHAPTER 12

A man does what he must - in spite of personal consequences, in spite of obstacles and dangers and pressures - and that is the basis of all human morality. -Winston Churchill

I'm in **#MonkMode** right now. What does that mean? It means no excuses, no slip ups, and no bullshit. It means work. It means focusing on those things that need my energy, not on anything else.

Focused.

Honed in.

Ready to go.

No distractions from my mission. It means its game time. And it's necessary. I slip up and lose focus just like anyone, but I know how to get things back on track. I'm stubborn and willful and I don't believe I need any help - but I do.

That's what **#MonkMode** is. It's the remedy I turn to when I've been lax and paid the price. I have lost some discipline, gained some weight, wasn't meeting my daily word-count, and lost my way a little bit. Not overall. I refuse to ever do that again.

But I fail. To err is human, and all that... It's okay to fail, but it is not okay to stay there. You can be knocked down but what you cannot do is stay on the ground. No matter how many times you fail, you have to keep getting up.

That's what this is, for me. It's me rising again, more serious than ever. I originally heard the concept from **@TexasDom1** on twitter, another FoE brother. The concept, I'm sure, has been appropriated by many.

It's doing away with unnecessary distractions so that more energy can be spent on that which matters most at the time. For me, that's getting my discipline back on track in every area of my life. It's a period of increased focus for a really good reason.

The thing is, I know this isn't the first and it won't be the last time I do this. I'll be doing these intense bursts of focus ad infinitum. I will continue to do what's necessary to grow closer to being the best, strongest version of myself. That includes daily discipline and fixing it when I fail.

That's what is required. This isn't a one and done deal. This path never ends, men. Get used to it now. If you want to be better you must do better, and do it over and over again. We all want to be great, but too many men get frustrated when they don't go from dud to stud after a little bit of effort. Greatness is just a lot of small things done well, someone once said, and that's the way you've got to see it.

This is a grind, day in and day out. There are plenty of rewards to be reaped, I can assure you, but you've got to earn those rewards. Don't expect to get them before you deserve them, and know that you won't deserve them unless you work for them.

This chapter is going to serve as the final installment of *The Work.* Your final assignment is to maintain the spirit of all the other challenges in this book, ad infinitum. Continue to speak out when you feel you should; be honest about who you are and where you stand, both to others and yourself; continue to work out regularly; continue doing things you've never done before and doing things that make you feel alive; keep spending time alone, listening to the voice inside of you that you alone hear; move ever onward working toward the realization of your mission in life; continue to curate your life, to allow only the best to stay; keep spending time with your brothers, learning from them and growing and eventually teaching those who come along later; cultivate the spirit of masculinity within you into eternity.

Be aware that this is only a basic understanding of the things that you should be doing as a man to reclaim who you should have been all along. I recommend from here that you take part in a bigger challenge such as **31DtM_**or **SoulCon**. If you haven't already found the brotherhood that I have blathered on about in this book, both 31DtM and

SoulCon have men's groups that do the challenges together. For 31DtM it's going to be **FoE**, for **SoulCon** it'll be the group of the same name.

Continue to stoke the fires of masculinity within you. Don't quit, don't give in to what the modern feminized culture would have you be. You are a lion, so roar! Authentic masculinity is toxic only to the weak.

CHAPTER 12.5

"I'm so proud of you!" she said, smiling widely.

"Thanks, babe," he said, beaming at her. "It feels kind of surreal..."

"I always knew you'd make it," she replied.

He leaned forward and kissed her long on the lips. She was so beautiful, he had to do it, crowd of people around or not. The sun shone brightly on that cool spring morning, casting warmth on the people standing outside of the building where the graduation ceremony had taken place.

His newly earned badge glinted, reflecting the light onto her face. He felt strong in his Class A's, ready to get to work. He'd been working toward this moment for years, and not that it was here he just couldn't stop smiling.

He picked her up in his arms, lifting and spinning her in circles effortlessly.

"Putemdownputmedownputmedown!" she said quickly.

He laughed and put her back on the ground. She'd never really like being picked up, but he had always thought she was cute when she freaked out.

He turned at the sound of the Chief's voice, "Glad you have you aboard." They shook hands, he felt proud and tall. More came through to shake hands and give congratulations. He shook hands with his fellow cadets, wishing them well in their careers, hoping to see some of them again someday.

This was far from the end, he knew. It was just one more step on their road of life. He was finally living up to being the man he'd always wanted to be. Not perfect, no; far from it. He still had a ways to go, but he was a far cry from the boy he had been.

The man turned to his family, still beaming. "Let's go get something to eat."

CHAPTER 13

I want to make something very clear before I end this book. Masculinity is not toxic in any way. So, when you are called toxic for being a masculine man you have a choice. You can either disregard, or wear it as a badge of honor. Let me explain.

You can disregard it because to be straight with you, the type of person that calls masculinity toxic is not the type of person that you need to listen to. They are deluded and indoctrinated into the leftist, feminist mindset that is so prevalent today.

You can also feel free to wear it as a badge of honor, because your masculine nature is only toxic to the weak and feeble in mind, body and spirit. Masculinity is only toxic to the dregs of society, the extremists who say that strength is the problem, not their own inability to grow stronger. It's because the light is anathema to the dark, and it always has been. For those who hide in the dark, the light burns them when it shines their direction.

Those are your choices.

Do not accept the title as they would have you receive it. You are not toxic by your very existence, only toxic to *them*.

So, whether you choose to disregard the term altogether, or you decide to wear it honorably because you know that by being called toxically masculine they are admitting that you are the opposite of them, and that is who you should be.

The Work: A List

1. Make a list of those things about you that need to change, and hold nothing back.
2. The next time you feel like something isn't sitting right with you, speak up. If someone is challenging you, stand your ground.
3. Set aside one hour today and use it solely to work out.
4. Do something fun or exciting that you've never done before.
5. Take one hour today to be silent and listen. No phone, no books, no radio, no internet. Just you.
6. What do you love doing that maybe you've been neglecting because of whatever excuse you could come up with? What is your mission? What steps can you take to start living it out? Figure it out. Write it down.
7. Read over the list from Chapter 1, add at least one more quality, habit, etc. about yourself that needs to change, and accept and internalize everything that is on the list as being part of you.
8. Remove the negative influences from your life. Do not waste time on people that don't give a shit about you, or that don't give a shit about themselves.
9. Find a man, or more than one, with whom you can swap notes. Forge a brotherhood and utilize it.
10. Write a list of every good quality that you pos-

sess. Don't hold back.

11. Do something that makes you feel alive.

12. Maintain the spirit of masculinity, *ad infinitum*.

Further reading and resources

Books:
The Holy Bible by God ;)
Mouth Breather by Jon Parker
31 Days to Masculinity by Hunter Drew
Sanction by Roman McClay
The Way of Men by Jack Donovan
Slaying Your Fear by Adam Lane Smith
Wild at Heart by John Eldredge
King, Warrior, Magician, Lover by Robert Moore & Douglas Gillette

Other:
The Fraternity of Excellence
Gibborim
SoulCon

This is far from an exhaustive list, just a few links that I think you may find helpful in your journey.

If you have a paperback copy of this book, and are interested in any of the above resources, just search them. If you have the kindle version, click the links!

If you have the paperback version and want the kindle version, the matchbook price is only 99 cents!!

Thanks for reading this book. Chances are that if you picked it up then you either hate men or you are a man in need of a change. I'm fully aware that this book is sort of disjointed in places. My brain works weird but in spite of that, I hope that you gleaned some value from reading it. If you did please let me know by hitting me up on **Twitter** and by leaving a review on **Amazon!**

If you did, are doing, the work then congratulations. You are in the minority. If you go on to continue to improve your life and to grow, you are in the extreme minority. Please let me know if you have any questions. I'm more than happy to help. The best place to contact me is on **Twitter.**

I send out regular updates and run giveaways through my email list. If you'd like to stay up to date about future books and projects, and take part in any future giveaways, sign up to the list here: **Jon Parker Author Email List**

OTHER BOOKS BY JON PARKER

Mouth Breather by Jon Parker
Read the sneak peek of this novel
on the next page!

Stay tuned to my social media and email list
for my upcoming fantasy trilogy-

The Chronicles of Power

Prologue

Sixth Grade

Blood pumping.
Fists flailing.
The boy in front of me had no idea what he was doing. He had been picking on a fifth grader - and a girl, no less. Boys shouldn't pick on girls. Not *because* they are girls, but because nine times out of ten they are physically weaker than the boy doing the bullying. My uncle had taught me that preying on those weaker than you was dishonorable.

I ducked. The boy had almost landed a punch. I saw the perfect opportunity as my legs began pushing my torso back into an upright standing position – and I took it. I let fly a hay-maker. I had seen men do it on YouTube. The receiver of *that* punch was nearly always done for.

The boy had no idea what he was doing. It wasn't as if I was a Kung-Fu warrior or anything but I knew how to throw a punch, which was apparently something lost on the red-haired kid in front of me.

Connection.

The boy's pale face contorted in shock and with the force of the blow landed. His freckles seemed to dance in the twisting of his expression. Before I knew it I was looking at the boy's back. Blood was slowly dripping from his mouth as he lay on the ground unconscious, a single tooth resting a few feet away.

Heart beating wildly, I almost couldn't believe what I had done. I stood under the Texas sun with eyes wide open. A wind picked up just then, rustling the green leaves on the huge oaks that had been planted randomly by some kids back in the sixties. The summer air smelled of sweat and blood. I heard a thunderclap from miles away.

My mind began working rapidly trying to figure out what to do next. Should I leave? Should I call a teacher? Should I call my mom? Oh, no - Mom.

What would she think? She was probably going to be furious with me. She was always saying that I had to avoid fighting. She said that fighting and being aggressive could end up causing me more pain than it was worth. But what else could I do? I had to do something to help that girl!

The girl.

I turned around to see her standing about ten feet behind me with her back against an oak. Tears were pouring down her face and she looked frightened. When she saw me turn toward her she looked directly into my eyes. The words "thank you" were uttered, but so silently that I only knew of their existence by the movement of her lips. She turned and darted off, ponytail bouncing back and forth as she ran.

I looked back at the boy lying face first in the dirt. The boy's red, shoulder length hair rested across the upturned side of his face, obscuring the bruise that was already forming there. He'd been *so* angry.

I didn't know why he had been picking on that girl or why he had been furious at me for telling him to stop. I wondered why he had suddenly begun swinging at me madly without any sense of where he wanted to hit.

I checked once more behind me, looking for the girl. She was nowhere to be seen. Regardless of the consequences, I knew I had done the right thing. Bullying others, especially those weaker than you, was wrong and it showed how weak *you* were. My uncle taught me that internal weakness, weakness of character, was much worse than being physically weak.

Before he could come to his senses, I grabbed my now dust-covered backpack, heavy with my school books. Hoisting it over my shoulder and with one last glance at the boy on the ground, whose face was now resting in a small pool of blood, I walked away.

Chapter One

The sound of my feet dragging along the sidewalk, while bothersome to others, had become something of a comfort to me. Just as the steady "*tch...tch...tch*" was soothing, so too were the newly dead corpses of once vibrantly green leaves. The sidewalk under the great oaks was littered with them, but the street to my left was practically clear, thanks to the work of the street sweeper. In the darkness of night, with the light from the street lamps reflecting off of the rain-soaked road, I was reminded of a painting I had once seen. That particular painting portrayed a colorful autumn night and a man and woman walking together with their dog. The similarity was not complete, though. After all, there was no beautiful girl walking with me tonight, and Misty, my pit bull, was at home.

As the wind picked up and the chill in the air deepened, I lifted the hood on my black, zipped up rain jacket. The memory of that painting, and watching her eyes light up at seeing it, was one that I doubted I would ever forget. Of course, she didn't know that I even had this memory of her. It felt to me as though I had taken something that didn't really belong to me, but the memory was important regardless of that, or maybe because of it. I hadn't gone up to her that night, as I wanted to do. I was too afraid.

Seeing her in my mind's eye was but a short

respite in the torrent of thoughts and emotions that came down on me more relentlessly even than the heaviest autumn rainfall in North Texas.

My uncle Rob, who had been overseas for the last seven months somewhere in the Middle East, had been declared MIA. When Mom had called earlier that afternoon to deliver the terrible news, I could hear the sorrow in her voice. She was barely able to get the message across through choked back sobs and quick, short breaths. At the time I had been standing at the edge of the lake behind the new high school. It didn't seem to me that it was as big as a lake should be, really, but that didn't make it any less damaging to my cell phone. The shock of the news had caused me to drop it right into the water.

I knew that I should go straight home but I just couldn't imagine seeing Mom in such a sad state. I was already in a dark enough place as it was without that. And besides, I knew she would just break down as soon as I walked in the door. So, instead of facing her, I had been walking, for what seemed like a very long time, around Angel Grove. It was early autumn, the first of October, and still the beginning of freshman year. The days were warm enough, and the nights nice and cool. That night, with the constant drizzle soaking me to the bone, it was especially unseasonably cold. The biting wind made it worse by numbing my face and causing my nose to run. Still, though, it was preferable to seeing Mom cry.

Not only would she be sad but she'd likely be furious, too. I hadn't bothered to go into the water after my cell phone. I hadn't asked someone else to use theirs, either. I had simply begun walking. It was all I could do not to run and keep running. I wanted to leave this town full of bad memories and at fifteen years old I considered just taking off for good on my own, but I couldn't do that to her.

She needed me. We were all each other had in the world, save for Uncle Rob, and now he was gone. Just like my father – gone. It made me angry. I was pissed that he had decided to reenlist when he had a family, albeit not really a normal one, that loved him and needed him back in Texas. I knew that Rob was nothing like my biological father, he was a much better man, but that didn't make his absence any easier. If anything it made it much worse. He was also the only thing like a father that I had ever known.

Rob had told me that he and my father had been close when they were kids. Rob was the younger of the two brothers by 18 months and the brothers hadn't actually grown apart until I was born. After my birth, it was said that my father had changed. They said that it was because my parents were so young when they had me. They said that 20 years old was too young. In reality, I knew it was because he was nothing more than a selfish asshole. Uncle Rob, in many ways, felt the rejection by his older brother just as much as I did, maybe more.

The snap of a twig behind me gave me a start and I came to a stop as I realized that my mouth was hanging slightly open. I snapped it shut defiantly.

"Hey, Mouth Breather." The voice, colder even than the chill night in which we stood, was all too familiar. I despised the boy to whom that voice belonged nearly as much as I hated the name "Mouth Breather." That nickname had been earned a few years ago after the owner of that voice had noticed my bad habit of leaving my mouth open while in thought. And I happened to be lost in thought quite often. The term was basically synonymous with "idiot" and more than anything I hated being called an idiot.

I turned around unhurriedly. It was never good to show your enemies that you were afraid. Rob had taught me that. The boy's red hair framed his sinister looking face in a way that made my skin tingle. The expression he wore could freeze boiling water. This kid had been taunting me for years, but I had learned to put up with it. Now, though, I was in no mood to be bothered by him or anyone else.

"What do you want, Fish?" I knew that Bradan hated that insult of a nickname just as much as I hated the name "Mouth Breather." The sneer that came to my face on the tail end of my words seemed to make Bradan's face contort slightly, a dangerous look passing through his eyes. It was gone as quickly as it came.

"I heard what happened, with your uncle. That's a real shame." That lack of concern in Bradan's voice made it clear that he didn't care at all about what had happened to my uncle. "You know, he probably got shot by those terrorists over there.

That's what happens to weaklings. Weaklings like you and your uncle make me sick."

I wasn't sure how I had maintained my composure as he spoke, but I knew for certain that I was going to make him sorry he had ever met me.

I took a step toward Fish, committing to a bloody end. Another step and my fists were clenched. The third step stopped me in my tracks.

The shadows behind Fish were shifting right before my eyes. At first, I didn't understand what was happening but it quickly hit me with an unrelenting force that it wasn't the shadows moving, *it was people.*

Three boys, two of which I didn't know, stepped out from a small stand of maple trees. Fish leaned back against the maple nearest him, chuckling softly. "You know what we do to weaklings, Mouth Breather, and the way I see it: You're the weakest of them all."

I flashed back to that afternoon in sixth grade when Fish had been bullying Lisa. The vision of leaving Fish knocked out on the ground less one tooth and some blood was vibrant.

"I don't think you're going to make it out of here on two feet, Mouth Breather." Fish was the kid that everyone else steered clear of. He wasn't unusually large, a couple inches taller than me, but most were afraid of him anyway. He had an air about him that reeked of emotional instability.

I wasn't afraid of him. I knew that Fish was just another kid with a sad story. Everyone had a sad story.

I wasn't afraid of Fish.

But this wasn't just Fish.

This was a four-on-one fight and I had no weapon to defend myself with. The adrenaline had been pumping through my body since the snap of that twig, now it felt as if my body was in overdrive.

I wouldn't be able to hold off all four of these boys and I knew that if I tried I would likely end up in the hospital. Or worse.

There was only one thing left to do: **run**.

Chapter Two

Fear.

My heart pounded heavily and my lungs screamed for air. The sound of my feet pounding the pavement echoed down the empty streets and through the dark corridors between houses. I had been running for at least three blocks and I didn't know where I was or how much longer I could stay ahead of Fish and the others.

Pain.

It was becoming too much. If I had paid more attention to my surroundings during while walking I'd know where I was or which direction to run. Unfortunately, I'd been absorbed in thought and had gotten a little lost.

I could hear the grunting and heavy breathing of the boys behind me. Stopping wasn't an option. I noticed another cross street racing swiftly toward me. I darted to the left down another long, dark road. My lungs and legs were on fire but I couldn't quit. I had to do something quickly or this night was going to get a whole lot worse for me.

Angel Grove High was just coming in to view as I followed the curve of the road around the end of a row of houses. The monolithic library rose into the night sky on the south side of the school. The high school was the only building on this stretch and I knew that if I didn't make it there and figure out some way to lose these guys or someone to help me then I would be dead.

Their panting was now louder than ever and their curses growing more violent.

It felt as though the school was pulling away from me as I put everything I had into reaching it. As dark as it was out, it seemed like my vision was growing even darker. All I could see was the single street lamp on the north side of the school creating a circle of light underneath it and dimly lighting the school's entrance. There were no lights on inside. I kept running. Ten more feet and I breached the sacred light of the street lamp. I felt fingertips brush my back. A loud, frustrated growl from behind.

The light bathed ground stretched on forever before me. I knew that the school would be locked up and that there would be no quick way in, but I had been hoping that a teacher or someone else would still be inside, and then maybe I could have yelled or screamed; I could have dove headlong through their classroom window. That would have surely stopped the boys behind me.

Maybe.

But it was just my luck that there would be no one still at school. I didn't even know how late it was and as this realization spread over me I began to understand just how foolhardy this half-plan had been. There was nothing left I could do. I began to think that the pain these fools would dish out couldn't be much worse than what I was already feeling. It might be best if I just stopped running and got it over with.

Passing through the light from the street lamp, plunged back into darkness, I looked around in one last ditch effort to find redemption from the executioners on my heels.

And then I saw it.

The lake; the lake where I had been when my mother told me about Uncle Rob; the lake where I had dropped my cell phone; the lake that everyone in the city of Angel Grove called "Demon Lake."

No one went in that lake.

No one.

Except for me.

The lake must have been more than a hundred yards to the south, but it was my only chance. Rumor had it that Fish couldn't swim, as ironic as that was. I knew that the boys chasing me wouldn't jump in there.

I hoped they wouldn't.

I raced across the parking lot on the west side of the school. It felt like with each step my feet were beginning to sink into the parking lot itself. My legs were heavy, my lungs in more pain than I had ever felt, my mind on the verge of giving up. But I couldn't.

I reached the edge of the parking lot and met a short wall, about 4 feet tall. I put my left hand out to place on top of the wall to hold my weight for a vault. Once there, I pushed off of the ground with all my might.

All of my might wasn't enough.

My left knee clipped the top of the wall, sending me careening toward the expanse of dirt on the other side. Time had slowed and at that moment, hanging in midair, facing the way I had come, I saw that the boys chasing me had fallen behind. They had stopped at the far edge of the parking lot. One was on his hands and knees, vomiting on the ground. Two were bent over at the waist, sucking air. Fish was standing tall, hands on his waist, breathing heavily, and glaring at me.

I saw his expression change as he realized that I was no longer on my feet. His eyes lit up and he screamed at the others to follow him as his feet began pulling him toward me.

I felt my chances of escape growing slim as the boys disappeared behind the height of the wall. I could feel the skin being shredded from my palm as my weight settled firmly onto my hand.

My wrist bent with a sickening crunch. It felt as if everything was taking a lifetime to happen; as if my life wasn't about to end.

My body began to grind into the ground, *hard*. The world came crashing in around me and the final act of the fall happened quickly. I felt the left side of my face rip open as it caught a jagged rock sticking up from the ground.

I landed some feet away from the wall. The pain made the distance feel much longer than it actually was.

I tried to climb to my feet but I couldn't make my arms work. I turned my head to see that the first boy who had jumped the wall had also fallen, though not as hard as I had. Fish was up and over the wall with fluidity.

He landed on the boy on the ground, who produced a clipped but loud screech of pain. The unsure footing brought Fish to the ground. The two boys behind him had seen the mess and had stopped short.

Fish, on his back on top of the other boy who had fallen, was only about ten feet away. I had to move. My right arm was useless.

My left arm, as much as it hurt, still seemed to be in working order. Adrenaline and willpower pushed me to my feet. I gingerly brushed the dirt and gravel from where it was stuck on the left side of my face, wincing in pain.

My hand came away wet and I felt a painful stinging well up in a line. Whatever it was I had no time to bother with it just then. Fish was climbing to his feet as well.

I cradled my right arm with my left and took off toward Demon Lake. I was sure that Fish wouldn't follow me in there, and since he was the leader of the gang of misfits chasing me I could be reasonably sure the others wouldn't go in either. Or they would, and I would likely drown.

I had no other option.

I turned my head to catch a quick glance behind me. I saw nothing but the red-faced rage monster chasing me. I felt his fingers grasp for the back of my shirt, nearly getting hold of it. I closed my eyes and ran with everything I had left in me. I lengthened my stride and pushed away from the ground with more force. All I could feel was the fire of fatigue and adrenaline coursing through my body.

I ran.

My fear, the fear that had been built on a desire not to suffer at the hands of the morons chasing me, had been compounded with each step as I made good my escape, or at least as I tried to. I was spurred on by fear, but Fish was propelled by something too. I didn't know why he was putting so much effort into catching me, and that made me even more afraid.

Water.

My eyes shot open as icy water enveloped my body. I had to fight not to breathe in as my body sank into the hypothermia-inducing waters. I hadn't been ready for the water and in fact, I didn't really even believe that I would make it that far.

The water by the bank was probably only eight feet deep or so, and I quickly found my footing and pushed off of the lake bottom. My head breached the surface and I gasped for air like my life depended on it – because it did.

Rowing with my working arm and kicking with my legs, I tried to tread water and to come up with a new plan that would give me respite from this ill-devised plan of escape.

Just then I heard wild splashing behind me. I turned in the water, feeling the pain of the fall that I had taken, the pain of the run, the pain of the cold water and air, the pain of my useless right arm.

There, about fifteen feet behind me was Fish.

I thought that he wouldn't follow me in! I thought that he couldn't swim! Fear gripped me tighter.

I could barely hold my head above water, how would I fight him off? I knew then that I was going to drown.

Frozen in more ways than one, I stared at the spot where Fish's head had just dipped below the water. The seconds dragged sluggishly on while I kicked my legs and waved my arm under the frigid waters of Demon Lake. Fish wasn't coming back up.

The three boys that had been with Fish had caught up. They were standing on the edge of the bank where it jutted out over the water's surface. They each appeared to be trying to catch their breath, not yet grasping the severity of the situation.

Panicking, I began moving through the water as swiftly as possible, making my way toward where I had last seen Fish. Nearly to the spot, I yelled out.

"Fish!!" I may have hated him, and he me, but that didn't mean I wanted him dead. I couldn't just do nothing as he drowned, not when I had the opportunity to help.

At the sound of my yelling, the boys on the bank realized that their leader wasn't anywhere to be seen.

"Where is Bradan?" It was the one that had attempted jumping over the wall before Fish; the one that had broken Fish's fall.

"He's underwater!"

I had been in the water for less than a minute at this point, but it felt as though my very bones were freezing. My limbs were growing stiffer by the second from the cold or the pain or the exhaustion. I wasn't sure which but I knew that I had to get out of the water as quickly as possible. The three boys continued standing on the bank, dumbfounded.

"Help me!" At my urging the one who had spoken jumped into the lake.

He didn't look like he was in very good shape after the fall he took moments before, but he definitely looked better than me. He quickly made his way to where I was, where I had seen Fish submerge moments earlier. "Derek, what are you doing!?" One of the boys still on the bank was yelling. I remembered this kid; Derek. I had spoken with him before.

Why is he chasing me with these idiots?

I dipped my head under, letting some of the air out of my lungs so that I would sink to the bottom quicker. Once my feet touched the bottom of the lake I opened my eyes. It was pitch black under the water. Unable to see anything I began feeling about with my good arm. I moved farther in the direction in which I thought that Fish might be, feeling randomly in front of me. It didn't take long for my lungs to start burning again.

When I surfaced I didn't see Derek. He must have still been underneath the water. Taking a few big gulps of the cold night air I dipped under again. I slowly released the air, as much as I dared, as I sank.

I didn't want to end up drowning down here myself. What a story that would be! It would be terrible for Mom, especially right now with Uncle Rob being MIA in wherever.

My wounds were becoming more painful by the second as I felt around aimlessly under the water. I squatted and pushed off of the lake bottom with my feet, propelling myself away from the bank. While this lake wasn't very big, it could still pull a body out away from land. After making it a good ten feet I slowed my momentum, swimming in small circles near the bottom. My hope was that I could cover a good amount of space before my air ran out.

No luck.

Feeling like my head was about to explode I set my feet down and prepared to push back to the surface. My arm brushed something. I reached out for it.

Cloth.

No – a shirt!

I grasped madly for the clothing. The pain in my head and lungs was building, compounding the already terrible aches all over my body. I had never experienced this level of pain. Nothing, not running miles around the school track, not sprinting down the football field repeatedly, nothing felt like this.

I didn't pace myself. I didn't stop. Everything in me had gone into escaping, and now here I was trying to save the life of my tormenter. My left hand gripping Bradan's shirt, I pushed away from the lake bottom one final time.

Air.

I was finally able to breathe. Joy filled me, riding on the coattails of the air I inhaled. Bradan didn't feel either of those things. The emotion in me evaporated with the realization that I wasn't going to be able to keep my head above water without the use of the arm that I was holding his shirt with. I kicked my legs with all of my might in an attempt to reach the bank.

If I let go of Fish then I would have been able to swim to land and save myself.

I didn't.

I couldn't.

My muscles were completely used up. I couldn't even have waved my hand, had I wanted to greet the lake-dwelling demons.

I held the cloth of Bradan's shirt tighter than I'd ever gripped anything before. I was simply unable to let him go. This would be my last night. Mom would be so sad; so angry. Maybe they would find Uncle Rob and Mom wouldn't be alone. Maybe he would be able to dry her tears...

The last bit of air escaped my lungs, forming bubbles that rose to the surface without worry for me. Broken fractals of moonlight found their way through the shifting, cursed waters of Demon Lake to dance across my vision. Maybe the lake really was haunted. If I hadn't jumped in, would I have escaped those boys chasing me? Would things be different now? Would I still have a chance at life?

I always loved books and stories. Too many of them described the act of death as the character being enveloped by darkness. I was loath to see that same darkness blot out my vision and take my consciousness from me.

If you'd like to read more, pick up a kindle or print version here:

Jon Parker Author Page

Made in the USA
Coppell, TX
04 February 2020